EASY RECIPES FOR THE HURRY HOME COOK

HEALTHY INDIAN
VEGETARIAN
COOKING

SHUBHRA RAMINENI

photography by Minori Kawana

TUTTLE Publishing

Tokyo | Rutland, Vermont | Singapore

Published by Tuttle Publishing, an imprint of
Periplus Editions (HK) Ltd.

www.tuttlepublishing.com

ISBN: 978-0-8048-4311-9

Distributed by
North America, Latin America & Europe
Tuttle Publishing
364 Innovation Drive
North Clarendon, VT 05759-9436 U.S.A.
Tel: 1 (802) 773-8930; Fax: 1 (802) 773-6993
info@tuttlepublishing.com
www.tuttlepublishing.com

Japan
Tuttle Publishing
Yaekari Building, 3rd Floor
5-4-12 Osaki; Shinagawa-ku
Tokyo 141-0032
Tel: (81) 3 5437-0171; Fax: (81) 3 5437-0755
sales@tuttle.co.jp
www.tuttle.co.jp

Asia Pacific
Berkeley Books Pte. Ltd.
61 Tai Seng Avenue, #02-12,
Singapore 534167
Tel: (65) 6280-1330; Fax: (65) 6280-6290
inquiries@periplus.com.sg
www.periplus.com

16 15 14 13
8 7 6 5 4 3 2 1

Printed in Singapore   1303 CP

Dedication

To my dear mother, Neelam Verma. When I told my mom I got my second book deal, her initial response was a fearful "Oh no!" She knew that my book deal meant a lot of work for her, in teaching me new recipes and going through the tedious task of standardizing measurements and using measuring tools. My mom cooks by sight instead of with exact measuring tools, which she finds unnecessary as they slow her down. Although she knew she had a busy time coming up, she was still excited for me, and she graciously took time to teach me her quick and easy recipes and to impart her nutritional knowledge to me as a dietician. Thank you Mom for letting me make a mess in your kitchen, and for your time, patience, knowledge, support, and love.

Acknowledgments

I would like to thank my dearest sweet husband, Naveen, for supporting and encouraging me every day in every way. Whether it's fixing a nerve-wracking computer malfunction, helping with the never-ending pile of dishes, caring for our darling daughter, or tasting and approving all of the fruit and vegetable dishes in this book, he is always there for me.

I want to thank my delightful daughter, Jaya, for always finding fun in every situation, even when I had to work long hours on my computer for this book. She would imitate me and bring her own toy computer and sit on her little table with a pencil, notebook, toy cell phone, and calculator. At the same time, she also had dishes cooking in her play kitchen while I was in my kitchen testing recipes.

I am also very appreciative of my dear friend, Anik Sayad Desjardins, who was there for me at a moment's notice, always willing to give a helping hand and sharing her culinary knowledge. Thanks for being a kind, amazing person and a wonderful friend.

Thank you Monica Pope for writing the foreword for my book. I am honored to have met you and to teach your Cooking Therapy classes along with you... such fun, organized chaos they are! I admire your efforts to be eco-conscious from recycling the oil in your restaurant kitchen to supporting local farmers.

I would like to thank my editor, Bud Sperry, my designer, Irene Ho, and my editorial supervisor, June Chong, for working with me on my vision of this book to come together beautifully. And for the amazing photographs in this book, a thank you to Minori Kawana. A heartfelt thanks to Rowan Muelling-Auer and Christopher Johns at Tuttle Publishing for your continuous support and for doing all the amazing things you both do.

Contents

Foreword by Monica Pope 8
Introduction 11
Enjoying Nature's Bounty 12
Kitchen Tools 16
Cooking Tips 19
Basic Techniques 20
Basic Ingredients 24

CHAPTER 1

Pickles and Chutneys 32
Spiced Yogurt with Potatoes 32
Pickled Turnips, Carrots and
 Cauliflower 34
Pickled Carrots 35
Pickled Beets 35
Roasted Peanut Chutney 36
Sweet and Spicy Pear Chutney 36
Fresh Coriander Chutney 37

CHAPTER 2

Appetizers and Snacks 38
Spiced Fruit Cocktail 40
Fresh Exotic Fruits 41
Grilled Vegetable Platter 42
Salted Fried Cashews 43
Pan-Seared Brussels Sprouts 44
Oven-Roasted Asparagus Spears 44
Indian Style Grilled Corn 45
Spinach and Fenugreek Fritters 46
Tomato Soup 47
Spicy Sweet Potatoes 48
Potato Cutlets 50
Opo Squash Fritters 51

CHAPTER 3

Breads and Rice 52
Baked Whole Wheat Flatbreads 54
Daikon Stuffed Wheat Flatbreads 56
Opo Squash Flatbreads 58
Quinoa Cashew Pilaf 60
Indian Cornbread 61
Fenugreek Cornbreads 62
Plain Basmati Rice 63
Rice with Cumin and Peas 64
Vegetable Pilaf Rice 65
Saffron, Fruit, and Nut Rice 66
Mint Rice 67

CHAPTER 4

Lentils and Legumes 68

Kidney Bean Curry 70
Black Bean Curry 71
Black-Eyed Pea Curry 72
Split Chickpea and Zucchini Stew 73
Green Lentils and Kale Stew 74
Buttery Black Lentil Stew 75
Stewed Whole Red Lentils 76
Stewed Split Red Lentils 77
Chickpea Curry 78
Fresh Lentil Sprout Salad 79

CHAPTER 5

Vegetable Main Dishes 80

Cut Bell Peppers and Potatoes 82
Mashed Turnips 83
Sweet and Spicy Butternut Squash 84
Curried Carrots and Peas 85
Green Beans with Potatoes 86
Spinach and Potatoes 87
Cauliflower and Potatoes 88
Sautéed Mushrooms and Peas 89
Sautéed Potatoes with Cumin 90
Yellow Squash Curry 91
Stuffed Okra 92
Fenugreek and Potatoes 93
Stuffed Bitter Melon 94
Opo Squash Dumpling Curry 95
Japanese Eggplants with Potatoes 96
Cabbage and Peas 97
Mixed Greens 98
Collard Greens and Parsnips 99

CHAPTER 6

Tofu and Cheese 100

Homemade Crumbled Indian Cheese 102
Vegetable Curry with Tofu 103
Indian Cheese Block 104
Indian Cheese and Pea Curry 106
Creamed Swiss Chard with
  Cheese Cubes 107
Cheese and Bell Pepper Skewers 108
Garam Masala 109
Pan-Fried Cheese Cubes 110
Tofu Breakfast Scramble 111
Indian Cheese with Peas 112
Tandoori Tofu Kebabs 113

CHAPTER 7

A Fruitful Ending:
  Drinks and Desserts 114

Strawberry Lassi 116
Fresh Vegetable Juice 117
Fresh Fruit Juice 117
Indian Cappuccino 118
Chai Tea 119
Melon Balls in Rose Syrup 120
Mango Ice Cream 121
Fruit Custard 122
Sweetened Carrots 123
Chocolate and Coconut Covered
  Cherries 124

Index 126
Resource Guides 128

Eat Where Your Food Lives

I had the pleasure of meeting Shubhra Ramineni at an event at my restaurant that the Bellaire, TX mothers group got together. For the last six years, I have been giving talks, cooking demonstrations and interactive cooking experiences in the hopes of spreading the word on our philosophy of "eat where your food lives." This mantra has a double meaning for me: 1) obviously buy, cook, and eat local food and 2) eat food that is truly alive in flavor and nutritional density. Shubhra immediately connected with the kind of food we made and mentioned she had a cookbook so we planned to do a cooking class together, using her book and our kitchen space. Shubhra has since done two classes with us and has hosted three more events, sharing her love and knowledge of Indian cooking and more and more incorporating the local pantry and her garden.

As we both have young daughters and are passionate about good food, we have bonded on every family's effort to keep bringing our families to the dinner table. I have had over the years many wonderful Indian cooking mentors. My first real culinary exploration was with making my own curry powder and garam masala (roasted spice mix). Having traveled extensively and also going to cooking school in London, England, it has exposed me to more diverse and wonderful ethnic foods. My hope for my own daughter is that she will be fearless in the food world and be comfortable at any dinner table in the world, eating the rich food traditions wherever she happens to land.

Shubhra's hope with this book is to encourage people to eat more healthy vegetarian foods using easy to find Indian spices to make the dishes delicious. She encourages people to shop at local farmers markets, supporting their community and local farmers that grow responsibly with organic and sustainable methods that are good for us and for the earth. Right now at the local farmers markets, we have wonderful daikon, Swiss chard, and Japanese eggplants! I love to run into people from different parts of the world and ask them what they're going to make with what they find!

Shubhra has met some wonderful farmers like Stacey Roussel from All We Need Farms and has gone to visit her farm with her daughter. Stacey is a very special mom, wife, and farmer who puts into her farm all the love and goodness she can. For me, Stacey has been a wonderful partner in growing inspiring food like fresh chickpeas, baby kale, and sweet potato vines that will easily find their way into Shubhra's recipes I'm sure!

If I had to "label" my food, I would call it "global comfort food with local ingredients" and I believe Shubhra's book will encourage people to discover new vegetables and fruits at the market and use her easy recipes to enjoy them. People don't always know what to do with the fresh fruits and veggies, or aren't inspired, but Shubhra's easy recipes give an option to enjoy them with easy to find Indian spices.

I've enjoyed cooking and sharing techniques and sources with Shubhra and I'm sure you will too! Enjoy her latest book and get into fruits and veggies and share with your family!

Sincerely,

Monica Pope
monicapopehouston.com

Enjoying an afternoon with my mom in her garden in Houston, TX.

Father and daughter plucking pomegranates from a tree in Atlanta, GA.

My hubby and me at an Indian restaurant in Austin, TX.

Dear Readers,

While working on my first cookbook, *Entice with Spice, Easy Indian Recipes for Busy People*, I knew my next book would be a healthy vegetarian cookbook. I have always had a great appreciation for a meatless diet because of its many health benefits. Having recently become a new mom, I am even more interested and encouraged to cook healthy dishes using fresh produce for my family. For two years I've been creating, cooking, and tasting recipes, and now I'm happy to share my collection of quick and easy, healthy, flavorful, and satisfying vegetarian recipes here.

This cookbook has a wide variety of recipes prepared from fresh fruits, vegetables, grains, nuts, lentils, legumes, tofu, and *paneer* (Indian homemade cheese) inspired by Indian cooking styles and flavors that I learned from my mother. My mom is not only a dietician but a fabulous gardener and a good cook as well. I am simply amazed at how she can prepare a nutritious and delicious dinner by picking vegetables grown in her own back yard and cooking them with Indian spices that have natural health benefits and healing properties.

As we continue to seek out healthier and sustainable lifestyles we have greater knowledge of our food sources and its implications and are leaning towards eating more fresh fruits and vegetables. However, many people may not have an idea of how to prepare and cook these fruits and vegetables. My recipes will enable you to cook scrumptious vegetarian and vegan dishes so you can enjoy incorporating fruits and vegetables into a healthy, balanced and wholesome diet.

I also wanted to share my experiences in shopping for, storing, and cutting up the fruits and vegetables you can find in your grocers, co-ops, farmers markets, and CSA's. I have included time-saving tips so you can cook and prepare ahead of time. I am certain that after cooking with this book, you will see fruits, nuts, vegetables, grains, lentils, legumes, tofu, and *paneer* in a different light. You will realize the fun, ease, and simplicity of cooking with them and will appreciate how nutritious, delectable, and environmentally friendly they can be. Even my three-year-old daughter enjoys eating her fruits and vegetables when I use them in these Indian-inspired recipes. I hope you will too!

Enjoy!

Shubhra Ramineni
www.enticewithspice.com

Enjoying Nature's Bounty

"I grew up on a predominantly vegetarian diet, and appreciate the freshness, health benefits, taste, and variety of meatless dishes that can be easily made. After having my daughter, I have become more aware of our food and the ingredients on food labels. I want to ensure that my family eats wholesome, natural foods. My daughter's love of vegetables led to my creating recipes to incorporate her favorite veggies, such as adding broccoli to my original Vegetable Rice Pilaf (page 65) dish."

Like my mother, one of my most enjoyable hobbies is gardening, and my daughter is following in my footsteps. I have learned some great growing tips from my mom for a bountiful garden full of tomatoes, opo squash, eggplants, and okra. It is so fun and rewarding to plant fruits and vegetables, watch them grow, and then harvest them and cook them into delicious dishes for my family and friends to savor. My daughter was so excited when she first saw the oranges on my tree growing bigger and bigger and even more excited when I plucked it for her and peeled it open for us to enjoy!

I find it so exciting when I cook and share vegetarian dishes with my friends from different ethnicities and they are pleasantly surprised at the ease of preparation and great flavors. My Indian friends also are amazed at how vegetables not native to Indian cuisine, such as collard greens and parsnips, can be cooked with Indian spices to create unique and tasty dishes.

Jaya is excited about these just delivered goods from Farmhouse Delivery.

A wonderful harvest of string beans.

Baby Jaya is picking the oranges from my potted tree.

With people becoming more health and environment conscious and more aware of where their food comes from and what is in it, cooking and eating more vegetarian meals prepared from fruits, vegetables, grains, nuts, lentils, legumes, tofu, and homemade cheese is becoming the norm of healthy living today. Whatever the reason for following the growing trend of vegetarianism, or at least reducing the amount of consumed meat (raised ethically and farmed humanely), there are definitely benefits for your health and the environment. Using Indian influences for cooking techniques and flavors, this book will guide you to easily making healthy and tasty vegetarian, vegan, and gluten-free dishes to dine on from breakfast to dinner and from appetizers to desserts. With my simple, nutritious recipes you can enjoy delicious, fresh, unprocessed food without hormones, preservatives, and other chemical pesticides and fertilizers. If you only have frozen vegetables on hand, feel free to use them as well.

Are You a Locavore?

You might be a locavore, and not even know it! Locavores are trying to support local farmers and the planet by being aware of where their food comes from in the world. Locally grown food has a shorter transportation distance, resulting in fresher food and fewer emissions in the environment.

Many people shop their neighborhood farmers markets and food cooperatives (co-ops) for fresh, locally grown seasonal produce, or are joining a Community Supported Agriculture (CSA) to receive weekly shares of farm-fresh fruits and vegetables. The contents of their bounty vary depending on seasonality and availability.

Locavores follow the slow food movement that encourages the enjoyment of regional produce that are often grown organically and by sustainable farming methods that protect and conserve natural resources.

Jaya and my mother picking tomatoes from my mother's garden.

My little gardener, Jaya, is meticulously watering my plants.

Chinese eggplants soak up the Indian spices and add color to a dish.

Baby Jaya eager to pluck ripening oranges.

Garam Masala…the fragrant roasted spice mix.

Oven-Roasted Asparagus Spears with roasted cumin and almonds.

If you were ever at a loss of how to prepare your fresh bounty of produce, this book will help to prepare the produce into delicious, flavorful, and satisfying dishes using Indian spices….perhaps juicy pears to make a delightful chutney to spread on your breakfast toast, tender yellow squash to make a spicy curry to enjoy with Basmati rice, or fragrant sweet mangoes to make an unforgettable ice cream for dessert, and so many more recipes for you to relish!

About Indian Spices

My recipes in this book use fresh fruits, vegetables, grains, nuts, lentils, legumes, tofu, and cheese that are prepared with Indian inspired techniques and flavors. Why Indian style? Because Indian food is traditionally vegetarian food, cooked with a variety of exotic spices, so it's the natural cuisine for delicious and healthy vegetarian food, including vegan and gluten-free dishes. Indian spices really give unique and wonderful tastes to dishes.

Some spices enhance the natural flavors of fruits and vegetables, while others jazz them up to make it an extravagant meal. Best of all, the spices incorporated in my recipes are easily accessible in most local grocery stores.

In addition to transforming a fruit or vegetable into an exotic delight, Indian spices have many healing properties and health benefits such as the anti-inflammatory property of turmeric to calm arthritis pain, heartburn relief from cardamom, tummy ache soothing from carom seeds, and much, much more.

If you are new to cooking with Indian spices, I would suggest starting off simply with five spices: salt, black pepper, ground red pepper (cayenne), cumin seeds, and ground turmeric. Find recipes in this book that just use those spices, and then you can build your spice collection with cloves, mustard seeds, cardamom, coriander seeds, saffron, and more. I cook with spices and ingredients that can be easily found at a local grocery store, without having to make special trips to ethnic markets.

Sautéed cauliflower and potatoes cooked with bright turmeric.

Cooking the everyday Indian whole wheat flatbread, Chapati.

Kidney Bean Curry spiced with Garam Masala.

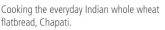

With a few easy to find spices, you just might be surprised at how easy it is to make healthy and delicious Indian inspired dishes that are quick and easy but taste and look like you went to some trouble! I myself am amazed at how one can take simple vegetables like green beans or okra and quickly turn them into wonderful and tasteful dishes using a few Indian spices. Even dishes made from vegetables not typically used in Indian cuisine, such as parsnips, butternut squash, jicama, and collard greens, are enhanced when using Indian spices and cooking techniques.

A Well-Balanced Meal and Life

A complete, healthy, and well balanced vegetarian meal can be served with the recipes in this book. You may start with a simple appetizer, continue with rice and/or bread, a vegetable dish, a lentil, legume, tofu, or cheese dish for the protein, a side of a spiced yogurt (*raita*), and finish with a beverage or dessert made with fresh fruits. Quick and easy one-pot meals such as my Vegetable Rice Pilaf (page 65)

can be offered with a side of plain yogurt for a well rounded meal. A simple meal of Plain Basmati Rice (page 63), a vegetable dish, and a lentil or legume dish served with a side of plain yogurt is an example of another quick and healthy weeknight meal. When pairing dishes to serve, I like to keep in mind the colors and consistencies for variety in taste and texture, and for beautiful presentation. A sautéed dish such as Cut Bell Peppers and Potatoes (page 82) goes well with a curry dish, which is a dish that has a saucy or liquid base such as Black-Eyed Pea Curry (page 72) or a soupy lentil dish such as Stewed Split Red Lentils (page 77).

With portion control, daily exercise, seven to eight hours of sleep per night, and good eating habits consisting of a diet full of delicious and nutritious vegetarian dishes, one can lead a healthy and active lifestyle. I hope to pass these healthy habits on to my daughter as my mom did to me. So go ahead and start having fun cooking delicious vegetarian, vegan, and gluten-free dishes and nourishing your body with fresh wholesome foods!

Kitchen Tools

If you come to my kitchen, you will see I have very basic cookware and tools that are sufficient for my no-fuss cooking style. Other than the basics of a good everyday paring knife, a chef's knife, and a set of stainless steel pots, pans, and skillets, including a good quality, safe nonstick skillet, here are some other tools I frequently use. Stainless steel is durable, dishwasher safe, and nonreactive to acidic ingredients such as tomatoes. I prefer to use heavy bottomed cookware since it gives me more control than thin pans do because the food does not heat up too quickly and possibly burn if you don't not keep a sharp eye on it, which I find hard to do with the distractions I get from my young child!

Blender/Immersion Blender
I like to have two types of blenders in my kitchen. The first is a traditional blender in which I make refreshing fruit smoothies and various chutneys. If you are using a blender to purée hot foods, let the food cool slightly before pouring it into the blender to avoid the lid popping open from the steam and creating a big mess.

The second type of blender I use is the immersion blender, also called a "hand blender." The immersion blender has a stick handle and a small metal blade at the bottom. You hold it in your hand and immerse it directly into the pot of food to be blended. This works great for puréeing spinach when I make Spinach and Potatoes (page 87) because I do not have to wait for the hot spinach to cool and then transfer it to a traditional blender. Instead, I simply immerse the hand blender directly into the hot pot and blend the spinach until smooth. To avoid splattering, try to keep the blender fully immersed in the food while you're using it.

Box Grater This tool is used to grate (shred) food. A typical box grater has four different sides, each with a different purpose. I use the side with the largest round grooves to grate onions and the side with the small grooves to grate ginger and carrots. You might see some other prickly holes that look like small pointed rasps, which I use to grate whole nutmeg. You can even zest lemons, limes, and oranges on this side. Some box graters also have raised, sharp horizontal slits that are used to get shavings of food, such as cheese and vegetables. To use a box grater, stand it on a plate or cutting board, hold the grater in place by firmly grabbing the handle with one hand, and grate the food by holding it in the other hand and move it up and down across the surface. Be careful not to scrape your knuckles!

Cast-Iron Skillet When making flatbreads, a cast-iron skillet works best. You need a surface that you can get quite hot and retains heat well. A cast-iron skillet can be seasoned over time (to create a smooth and safe nonstick surface) by repeatedly heating up the skillet and coating it with cooking oil. A cast-iron skillet should be gently scrubbed with water only and immediately dried to prevent rusting. An Indian rimless cast-iron skillet is a *tawa*, also spelled *tava* or *tawah*. *Tawa* are commonly either 10 or 12 inches (25 to 30.5 cm) in diameter. It is slightly curved and used to make various types of Indian flatbread. I find that using my low-rimmed American cast-iron skillet works just as well.

Cheesecloth Cheesecloth is a lightweight, cotton gauze that is traditionally used in cheese making. The cloth allows the whey to quickly drain out, while retaining the curds, creating the Indian cheese called *paneer*. You can also use it to strain tamarind pulp and coconut milk if you want to extract them from whole tamarind and fresh coconuts. Cheesecloth is found in various departments of grocery stores. If you do not have cheese cloth, you may use a thin muslin cloth instead. The size of your cheesecloth does not matter—as long as you can fold it at least four times so you do not lose the curds. Do not cut the cheesecloth if it seems too large, since a big piece is easy for lining a colander and has enough excess cloth to hang over the edge. After using a cheesecloth, wash it by rinsing any food products off it, and then use a few drops of dishwashing liquid and rub it in the cheesecloth. Rinse the soap off thoroughly and hang outside on a line to dry, or drape it over a dish rack on your counter, or in an empty rack in your dishwasher.

Food Processor, mini This compact version of a big food processor is small and simple, with just a basic two-prong blade. I can easily shred onions with it and make Fresh Coriander Chutney (page 37) in a flash. Although some foods can be similarly processed in a blender, a blender is typically used to purée liquids or items with a soupy consistency. A food processor allows for more cuts than a blender, depending on the blade used. For the recipes in this book, a simple, mini food processor with just the basic blade and a low and high speed button will do fine. I do a lot of grating of onions, and that can be done with this mini food processor instead of a box grater.

Juicer A juicer is a fun tool to extract the juice from the pulp of fruits and vegetables, including leafy greens such as spinach. Juicers come in manual and electric models; the manual ones being good for juicing citrus fruits such as oranges or grapefruits. But since I also like to juice fruits such as pineapple, and vegetables such as spinach and carrots, an electric juicer is ideal.

Citrus Squeezer Small-sized citrus squeezers are used to squeeze lemons and limes, and sometimes they are big enough to handle oranges too. You can find sturdy metal ones at household stores, kitchenware stores, and sometimes even in grocery stores. If you do not have a citrus squeezer, you can squeeze citrus fruits by hand over a small strainer to catch the seeds. When using the citrus squeezer, place half of the lemon or lime face down in the squeezer towards the holes so the juice will come out and press the handles. A common mistake when using a squeezer is to place the cut fruit the wrong way, which will cause the juice to splash out the sides of the squeezer.

Cutting Board It is best to get a cutting board that is made with smooth plastic or composite material such as polypropylene rather than the glass ones with a grooved surface. The latter are bad for knives and can dull them quickly. A wooden board is also good to use, especially for fruits and vegetables, since you do not have to worry about washing away any bacteria from meat by immersing the board in water, which damages the board. Wooden boards should be wiped clean with a damp cloth.

Garlic Press This tool makes fast work of mincing garlic. It is usually made of metal and presses peeled or unpeeled garlic cloves through small holes, creating a close substitute for hand-minced garlic. Although this tool saves time, I have found the downside is that it can be hard to clean out since garlic can get stuck in the grooves. After using it, be sure to pry out any garlic stuck in the press so it does not go to waste.

Immersion Blender (see Blender)

Mortar and Pestle A mortar and pestle is the traditional Indian tool used to crush and grind spices. It has a bowl-shaped base (the mortar) and a small bat-shaped stick (the pestle) that is used to crush the spices by repeatedly and forcefully pressing down on them while rotating the pestle. Mortars and pestles come in different sizes and materials, from marble or other stone, to wood, porcelain or metals. For all but very small amounts of spice or nuts, I prefer to use an electric coffee/spice grinder because it is faster. If you don't have a mortar and pestle, you can crush small amounts of spices or nuts by placing them in a plastic bag and, with the bag on a cutting board, tapping it with a rolling pin.

Parchment Paper This is a nonstick paper that is used in baking. I place a small piece between hot breads before freezing them so they will not stick to each other and tear or break when separating them for thawing and reheating. Even if the breads are very hot, they will not stick to the parchment when frozen. Parchment paper can be found in the same section of the grocery store where aluminum foil is found.

Rolling Pins I use mine to not only roll out dough, but I also use it to crush nuts and cardamom seeds and to ground up roasted cumin seeds. Rolling pins come in different material, such as metal, marble, silicon, and plastic. I prefer to use a wooden one because they are easy to find, relatively lightweight, and easy to clean. Tapered rolling pins can be pivoted and rotated while rolling out dough, which is very helpful when trying to roll out a perfect circle of dough.

Spice Grinder This handy gadget, also called a coffee grinder, can be used to grind spices, and definitely beats using a mortar and pestle—the traditional tool for grinding spices. From my experience, I have seen the motor burn out if you overload the spice grinder, or run it for a long time at one stretch. It is best to grind spices in small batches, and frequently rest the motor for a few seconds while operating it. To clean the spice grinder, I take a damp paper towel and carefully and slowly wipe the inside and the blade. You may also grind some uncooked white rice in the grinder so the spice aromas will be absorbed by the rice.

Sieve, also called strainer A sieve is a type of handheld strainer made of wire mesh that allows liquids to pass through, while keeping the solids in the strainer. They come in different sizes, from small to large. I use a small strainer when making Chai Tea (page 119) to collect the cardamom pods and seeds and the tea bags. I use a large sieve when making Tomato Soup (page 47) and also to squeeze out the liquid from the grated opo squash to make Opo Squash Fritters (page 51). A large sieve is also a great tool for washing rice and lentils without having to worry about losing any grains or lentils down the sink!

Spider Also called a wire skimmer, this tool gets its name because of its resemblance to a spider's web. At one end of a long handle is a broad, circular, shallow bowl of loosely spaced, but sturdy wire mesh. The spider can be use to scoop up and strain a wide variety of ingredients such as vegetables or pasta in a boiling pot of water, or anything deep-fried. I especially like to use this tool when

making Salted Fried Cashews (page 43), since I can put a batch of cashews in the spider, safely lower it into the hot oil, and then quickly raise the spider back up when the cashews are done.

Wok A wok is a round-bottomed cooking utensil popular in Asian cooking for stir-frying. It can be used to efficiently deep-fry, since the round bottom shape creates a deeper frying area that requires less oil than a flat-bottomed pot with straight sides. A *karahi* is an Indian wok that is used to deep-fry foods. The bottom of a *karahi* is not as rounded as a Chinese wok, but it is still an efficient utensil to deep-fry foods. If you prefer to get an Indian wok, they are sometimes available at Indian grocery stores, or you can order them online.

Cooking Tips

Here are some of my basic cooking tips that I would like to share with you to make cooking in the kitchen an easier, quicker, and more fun experience.

❀ Plan ahead. Cook one or two days a week and refrigerate or freeze the food so that you can have dinner ready quickly after a long day at work. Each recipe has refrigeration, freezing, and reheating tips to ensure you have a delicious meal ready to enjoy.

❀ When you're ready to freeze a dish, make sure the hot food has cooled to room temperature, especially before putting it into plastic containers or in freezer-safe plastic bags, and place in the freezer for up to one month. Make sure the container is well covered or airtight so that ice crystals won't form on the food. The easiest way to reheat frozen food is to first thaw it by placing it in the refrigerator, and then warming it up in the microwave or on the stovetop. You can also use a microwave to defrost the food.

❀ Make a few cups of Plain Basmati Rice (page 63) or Rice with Cumin and Peas (page 64) every weekend so you have it on hand during the week to eat with your meals. For perfect rice that is not mushy, do not cook more than 2 cups (360 g) of rice at one time.

❀ If you are new to cooking with Indian spices, I would suggest starting off with recipes that use these five basic spices: salt, black pepper, ground red pepper (cayenne), cumin seeds, and ground turmeric. Then you can build your spice collection with spices such as cloves, cardamom, coriander seeds, and saffron.

❀ Normally, food will thicken when chilled, but when reheated it will return to its original consistency. If the food is still thick after being reheated, simply add some water to thin it out.

❀ Do not double or triple a recipe until you get used to making the recipe, especially the rice dishes.

❀ If a recipe calls for a lime, you can use a lemon instead if that is all you have on hand. I use limes since they are less expensive and easier to find. If a recipe calls for the juice of one lime, you can also use the juice of one-half lemon instead (since lemons are bigger than limes). If you prefer to use key limes, you can use two of those to equal one lime.

❀ If you accidentally add cumin seeds to an overheated pan or if you cook them too long in oil and they burn, discard them along with the oil and start again. Burnt cumin seeds will ruin the taste of your dish and they are unsightly.

❀ Canola and peanut oils are better than vegetable oil for frying since they have higher smoke points (the temperature at which the oil starts to emit smoke and unpleasant odors, resulting in poor flavor and burning).

❀ Always use fully ripe, soft, red tomatoes for quicker cooking times, the best flavor, and for their beautiful deep red color. In the cooking process, tomato skins usually separate from the flesh. For better presentation, I often remove the big pieces of loose tomato skins before serving the dish. I prefer not to cut up the tomato into many small pieces, since that means the cooked dish will have many tiny tomato skins in it that would be hard to pick out.

❀ I cook with yellow onions since they are readily available and provide a nice flavor to food. Red onions are slightly sweet and white onions are milder than yellow onions, but you may use any variety you prefer. There are different stages of cooking onions, from becoming translucent to a golden brown, brown, dark brown, and finally to the point of caramelizing them, when the natural sugars cook and lend a sweet taste. Always cut or shred onions right before you are ready to cook them so they do not sit for too long and start releasing their water and smell bad.

❀ I have provided measurements in both American and metric units. Measurements don't have to be exact so don't stress about measuring ingredients precisely. Do note that the metric measurements are rounded so you can easily measure the ingredients; also note that I use a standard 250-milliliter equivalent when using cup measurements.

❀ My cooking times are based on using heavy cookware over a gas stove. Light cookware can be used, and is beneficial in the sense the food will cook faster; however, you have to keep a sharp eye on it and stir the food more frequently.

❀ If the recipe calls for a nonstick skillet, but you prefer to use a skillet without a nonstick surface, add an additional tablespoon of oil and stir the food more frequently. If your skillet it not heavy bottomed, you may also need to lower the heat to keep the food from burning. However, when pan-frying tofu, *paneer*, or potato cubes, the best results come with using a nonstick skillet. If I do not specify in a recipe that a nonstick skillet should be used, such as when roasting or tempering spices, then you can use either a nonstick or stainless-steel skillet

❀ I use plain iodized table salt in all of my recipes. Salt to taste. You may also use kosher salt or sea salt if you prefer. Both are coarser than table salt, so you will need to add a pinch or so more that what is indicated in the recipes for equal seasoning.

❀ You can control the fiery spice level in dishes by decreasing or increasing the amount of ground red pepper (cayenne), dried red chili peppers, or fresh green chili peppers used in the recipes.

❀ If a recipe calls for yogurt, you may use fat free, reduced fat, or regular yogurt. Make sure the yogurt is plain yogurt and not Greek yogurt or a flavored yogurt. You may also plain soy yogurt as a dairy-free, vegan substitute.

❀ To prevent cut or cubed potato pieces from browning, immerse in a bowl of cold water until ready to use.

Basic Techniques

If you run across a recipe and wonder how to cut a carrot into matchsticks, deal with a whole garlic bulb, roast spices, or even the difference between cubing, dicing, chopping and mincing, this section is the place to find the answers!

Roasting, Grinding, and Peeling Whole Spices

Cardamom Pods

To open a cardamom pod, place it on a cutting board. Place a small knife on its side flat on top of the cardamom and press on the knife to crack the pod open. Pry it apart with your fingers and remove the black seeds.

If you need to crush the seeds for a recipe, use a mortar and pestle to coarsely crush the seeds. Alternatively, put the seeds in a plastic bag. Put the bag on a cutting board and hit with a rolling pin until the seeds are coarsely crushed.

Roasting Whole Spices

Roasting spices is a common Indian technique used to deepen and bring out the flavors of the spices. The intense aroma given off by the spices while roasting and grinding them is amazing! It is best to roast and grind spices just when you plan to use them, since they lose their potency over time.

1 Place a small skillet over medium heat. When the skillet is heated, add the whole spices. Roast the spices until they are fragrant, stirring frequently, about 2 minutes. (Roast cumin seeds until they are dark brown, but not burnt.) Transfer the spices to a bowl and let cool before grinding.
2 Place the spices in a mortar and pestle and grind to a fine powder. Alternatively, put the spices on a small piece of foil, fold the foil over the seeds, and roll a rolling pin over them to crush the spices into a fine powder. You can also use an electric coffee or spice grinder. (In some recipes, spices are ground without roasting, such as mustard seeds.)
3 Use now or place in an airtight container at room temperature for up to 3 months.

Freezing Raw Vegetables

Fresh vegetables may be frozen if you will not be able to use them soon. My mother always has more tomatoes than she can cook in her garden, so she simply washes them and puts them in freezer-safe plastic bags and places it in her freezer for up to a month. When she is ready to cook with them, she thaws them by bringing them out at room temperature, and then she cooks with them. Similarly, most vegetables may be frozen such as okra, eggplant, and opo squash. You may freeze these vegetables whole, without cutting them up. Blanching is used to set the color and flavor of vegetables before freezing, but I do not find it necessary.

Preparing Dried Beans

Kidney beans, chickpeas, black beans, and black-eyed peas.

1 Place the dried beans on a plate. Sift through them and remove any grit or blemished beans.

2 Transfer the beans to a large bowl. Rinse the beans three times by repeatedly filling the bowl with cold water and carefully draining off the water. Add cold water to cover the beans. Discard any beans that float to the top of the water. Cover the bowl and let soak overnight at room temperature to allow the beans to expand and become tender.

3 The next morning, place a colander in the sink. Pour the soaked beans into the colander and rinse thoroughly.

4 Place the drained beans, 4 cups (1 liter) water and ¾ teaspoon salt in a large saucepan. Bring to a rolling boil over high heat. It is okay if the water gets frothy. (For kidney beans use 5 cups (1.25 liters) of water.)

5 Reduce the heat to medium-low. Cover the saucepan. Simmer until the beans are very soft, stirring occasionally, about 1 hour.

6 Keep 2 cups (500 ml) of the cooking liquid (broth) and discard the rest. If for some reason you do not have at least 2 cups (500 ml) of the cooking liquid, add some water to make up the balance. (For black-eyed peas keep 1½ cups (375 ml) of the cooking liquid.)

Blanching and Slivering Almonds

Though referred to as "nuts," almonds are actually the dry fruit from the almond tree. In this book, I use almonds that have been blanched and slivered, which means the brown skin has been removed (blanched) and the almond is sliced into thin longitudinal strips (slivered). Blanched and slivered almonds are usually found in small clear packets in the baking section of grocery stores. If you do not find them, it's easy to blanch whole almonds at home as described here. My mother tells me eating almonds improves your memory, and that it is good to eat a few daily. She soaks them overnight in water, peels and eats them along with her breakfast.

To blanch almonds, immerse them in a small bowl of water and microwave them on normal level for 1 minute. Let them cool and then remove the skin with your fingers (the skin should easily slip off). You can also immerse the almonds in water in a small saucepan and boil them on the stovetop for two minutes. Let them cool and then slip the skin off with your fingers. Alternatively, let the almonds sit overnight at room temperature in a small bowl with water. In the morning the almonds will be puffed up and tender, and the skin can be easily slipped off with your fingers.

To sliver the blanched almonds, place an almond on a cutting board and use a knife to cut the almond lengthwise into thin strips. Repeat with the other almonds.

Grating, Chopping, and Peeling

Ginger

Using the sharp edge of a small knife or the side edge of a small spoon, scrape off the thin tan skin from just the amount of ginger you want to grate. Grate it using a microplane or on the small holes of a box grater.

Grating

Grating means to shred, and produce, like onions, carrots and ginger can be grated. It can be done using a box grater or mini food processor. Before grating, peel the onion, ginger or carrot (peeling carrots is optional). Use the largest holes on a box grater for onions, and the smaller holes for carrots and ginger (see Box Grater on page 16). A microplane can be used for grating ginger as well. Remember to grate onions just before ready to cook them so they will not smell bad.

Garlic

To chop or mince fresh garlic, first pry off a clove from the garlic bulb with your fingers or by carefully using the tip of a small knife. Place the clove (with the peel on) on a cutting board and lay the side of a chef's knife flat on a clove with the blade facing away from you. Then firmly push down on the knife to smash the clove, which makes it easy to remove the papery white peel. After removing the peel with your fingers, mince or chop the clove with a knife, or you can use a garlic press (and with some presses you don't even need to take the peel off). You can also grate the peeled garlic clove using a microplane or on the small holes of a box grater.

Chopping and Mincing

Chopped food is bite-size or smaller pieces, and minced food is cut into very small pieces (smaller than diced), almost to the point where the food seems crushed, such as minced garlic or minced onion. Mincing food is handy when you do not want to bite into a big piece of garlic or onion, but you would still like your dish to have the flavor evenly dispersed. Mincing garlic can also be done using a garlic press.

Boiling the Potatoes

Boiling potatoes are an easy task, but you do have to factor in the half hour it will take when making a recipe that will use them.

1 Wash the unpeeled potatoes with cold water. In a large pot, add the potatoes, covering them with about 1 inch (2.5 cm) of water. Make sure that the level of the water is at least 2 inches (5 cm) from the top of the pot so that the water does not boil over.
2 Cover the pot. Bring to a rolling boil over high heat. Reduce the heat to medium-high and continue boiling for about 30 minutes, or until you can easily insert a knife into the potato. (Make sure you do not boil them to the point where they become too tender and easily fall apart, especially if you are going to cube or dice them.)
3 Drain the potatoes in a colander and let the potatoes cool slightly so you can handle them, or you can run cold water over them to cool them faster.
4 Using your fingers or a small knife, peel the skin off the potato and discard. The potatoes are now ready to be used in a recipe, or cover and refrigerate them up to 1 day.

NOTE: You may boil the potatoes up to one day in advance. They may be refrigerated already peeled or with the peels on, though it is easier to peel the skin off potatoes when they're still warm.

Cutting Methods

Fresh Cauliflower

The first time I prepared fresh cauliflower at home without my mother by my side, I was not sure how to cut it. For those new to using fresh cauliflower, here is how to cut it into florets:

1 Pull away the green leaves and discard. Using a small knife, gently scrape away any brown marks on the cauliflower head.
2 Slice off the stem at the bottom of the cauliflower head and discard.
3 Turn the head upside down so that it is stem-side up. Insert a small knife inside the head right next to the core to cut loose the florets from all around the internal stem (core). (The core can be chopped and enjoyed raw or it may be chopped and cooked along with the florets.)
4 Cut all the loose florets into small bite-size pieces.
5 Place the florets in a colander and wash with cold water.

Half-moons

Sometimes I specify a "half-moon" cut for onions, which is a semi-circle made by slicing an onion crosswise into rings, and then cutting the rings in half to create half-moons. Or, an onion may be cut lengthwise in half, and then both halves should be thinly sliced across to create half-moons.

Fresh Broccoli

1 Cut off any leaves on the broccoli stalk and discard.
2 Cut off the thicker bottom portion of the stalk. (The stalk can be peeled and chopped and cooked along with the florets.) You will now be left with the crown of the broccoli.
3 Use a small knife to separate the crown into individual florets. If some of the florets are big, cut them gently through the stem.

Cubes and Dice

The standard size cube size is ½ inch (1.25 cm) or larger. It is okay if all of the cubes are not exact squares, or if they have some rounded sides, but try to cut almost equal-size pieces so that the food cooks at an even rate. When a recipe calls for an ingredient to be diced, cut it into small cubes that are approximately ¼ inch (6 mm) or smaller. When a recipe calls for something such as green chili peppers or onions to be finely diced, the pieces are cut even smaller.

Matchsticks

Vegetables such as carrots and potatoes are commonly cut into strips called matchsticks, but usually not as thin as an actual matchstick. When creating thin matchsticks, the cut is known as "julienne." The vegetable is first cut into thin slices, and then the slices are cut across to the desired length, resulting in a short or long "matchstick." I like to use this attractive cut when preparing the carrots for Vegetable Rice Pilaf (page 65) and Vegetable Curry with Tofu (page 103).

1 Cut off the both ends of the carrot and discard.
2 Thinly peel off the outer skin and discard and then wash the carrot with cold water. Or you can leave the nutrient-rich peel on and thoroughly scrub the carrot with your hands or a vegetable brush.
3 Cut the carrot in half crosswise to make it an easier size to work with.
4 Cut each half lengthwise down the middle.
5 Cut each piece in half lengthwise again. For the thicker part of a carrot, you might want to make another lengthwise cut to create strips of even size.
6 Stack the strips and cut them crosswise into approximately 2-inches (5 cm) long matchsticks.

Basic Ingredients

Here I explain the magical and exotic, yet easy to find ingredients and spices, which will transform fruits, vegetables, and tofu into delicious dishes and will provide excellent health benefits as well. I use easily available ingredients that can be found at your local grocery store so you can conveniently make any dish in this book.

All-purpose flour is made from a blend of high-gluten hard wheat and low-gluten soft wheat. This fine textured flour is milled from the endosperm (inner part) of the wheat kernel and does not contain the germ (the sprouting part) nor the bran (the outer coating), which are nutrient and fiber rich parts of the kernel.

In America, the law requires all flours not containing the wheat germ must have niacin, riboflavin, thiamin, and iron added, thus making them "enriched" as the label on the package might say.

All-purpose flour is white in color and is sold as either bleached (naturally as it ages or chemically) or un-bleached, and both can be used interchangeably for a recipe. I use non self-rising flour, which means baking powder and salt have not been added.

Basmati rice is a long-grained, fragrant, gluten-free rice that is grown in the cool foothills of the Himalayan mountains in India. In Hindi, *basmati* means "the fragrant one," so the name seems to fit quite well. Basmati rice is commonly available in most grocery stores in small packages, and many international food stores sell big burlap sacks of basmati rice, which is more economical if you cook rice often like I do. Rice can be stored in a jar, plastic bag, or in the burlap bag it came in for at least six months in your pantry. But I like to store rice in my freezer so it keeps well and takes care of any bugs that may be in it from the store. It is a good idea to thoroughly wash the rice before cooking it to clean it and to remove any starchy residue so that the final result is less sticky. In general, the rule of thumb to cook basmati rice is to use twice the amount of water to rice. One cup of uncooked rice yields about three cups of cooked rice. Basmati rice comes in white and brown forms and you may use either for cooking, although I prefer to use white rice since I prefer its taste and texture. Rice is cholesterol and gluten-free, and a good source of fiber, which is good for a healthy and regular digestive system. *See also* Brown rice (page 25).

Bay leaves come fresh or dried, but dried bay leaves are easy to find and keep well, especially if one does not cook with them too often. When cooking, the leaf is added to heated oil or butter to release its sweet and woody aroma. I put bay leaves in my Vegetable Rice Pilaf (page 65). You may leave the bay leaf in your dish for presentation purposes, but with its sharp dried edges, it is best to avoid eating it. Drinking an infusion of bay leaves helps relieve upset stomachs and digestive disorders.

Black pepper (ground and whole peppercorns) is a berry that grows in grapelike clusters on the pepper plant. The berries can become green, black, or white peppercorns depending on how ripe the berry is when it is plucked and how it is processed. The black peppercorns have the strongest flavor whereas the white ones are milder and are used when you do not want the black pepper to show in food, such as a white sauce. The green berries are unripe when plucked and are commonly preserved in brine or pickled for a fresh taste. For everyday cooking, I use the finely ground black pepper that comes in a tin or I sometimes if I have time, I use freshly ground whole peppercorns. For some dishes, like Vegetable Rice Pilaf (page 65), I prefer to use whole black peppercorns that I temper in oil to release their flavors. Black pepper has antimicrobial properties that help destroy

---

Storage and Food Handling Tips When shopping for ingredients, I tend to buy small quantities so they will stay fresh, but when shopping for rice, I buy big burlap bags of it since I cook it often. You can store all of your individual spices, lentils, dried legumes, and rice in airtight jars in a cool, dry place and out of direct sun for up to six months. I actually like to store rice in the freezer in order to eliminate any bugs in it, since rice is prone to bugs from the warehouse. Flours are best kept up to three months in the pantry, but they may also be placed in the freezer for up to six months. Roasted and ground spice blends, such as Garam Masala (page 109), lose their flavors more quickly and are also best if kept up to three months only. Nuts have oils in them, which can cause them to go rancid if stored at room temperature. It is ideal to store nuts up to three to six months in the refrigerator or up to one year in the freezer. When handling spices, rice, lentils, dried legumes, flour, and nuts, always use dry hands and utensils when removing them from or adding them to storage containers.

cold-causing germs. This spice also helps relieve congestion by breaking up excess mucus and clearing nasal passages.

Brown rice is a gluten-free whole grain rice with only the inedible outer husk removed, unlike white rice, which has the husk, bran, and germ removed. This makes brown rice more nutritious than white rice, and also more effective in lowering cholesterol levels. The nutritious, high-fiber bran coating to brown rice gives it a light tan color, nutlike flavor, and chewy texture. The presence of bran limits the storage life of brown rice to six months since it can go rancid, but it may be refrigerated to extend its life. Brown rice may be substituted for recipes that call for white rice, but it does require more water and it takes longer to cook since it is the entire grain. Basmati rice comes in brown rice as well.

Cardamom come from the cardamom pods that are the fruit of the cardamom plant, and they are plucked while they are still unripe and then dried. The common variety is the small green pods with its warm, fragrant, and spicy-sweet intensely flavored small black seeds inside, which is what I use. There are also big black cardamom pods. If you shop in ethnic markets, you may also see small white cardamoms, which are simply the green ones that have been bleached for aesthetic purposes. Cardamom is frequently used to add a special touch to Indian desserts and tea. (See page 20 for instructions on how to work with cardamom pods.) My two-year-old daughter loves to chew on cardamom pods! Cardamom pods make good natural breath fresheners. Simply pop a whole pod in your mouth and chew on it until you can swallow everything. Cardamom also provides relief from heartburn.

Chili peppers, green (fresh, whole) There are hundreds of varieties of chili peppers, varying in length, thickness and spice level. Generally, the smaller a pepper, the hotter it is because there are more seeds proportionally, and the seeds are the heat source. In Indian cooking, many types of chili peppers are used, but I use the spicy hot bird's-eye chili pepper (also sometimes referred to as the "Thai chili pepper"). The bird's-eye chili pepper is thin and can be found in ethnic markets and now also in many American grocery stores. You can use any variety of green chili pepper, as I also frequently use the easily available Serrano chili pepper or jalapeño pepper. The Serrano and jalapeño are a bit bigger and plumper than the Indian bird's-eye, but they will still do fine. Capsaicin, the active component of chili peppers that gives them the fiery hot flavor is mainly in the seeds, so cutting open and chopping a chili pepper exposes the seeds and allows it to release more flavor and heat. Always make sure to wash your hands thoroughly after handling a chili pepper so you do not irritate your eyes, nose, or lips if you touch them afterwards. When green chili peppers are left on the plant long enough to fully ripen, they turn red and are then plucked and dried in the sun for use in cooking. Chili peppers provide pain relief, as studies have shown that capsaicin relieves and prevents headaches, including migraines.

Fresh green bird's-eye chili pepper

Chili peppers, red (dried, whole) Red chili peppers are green chili peppers that have been allowed to fully ripen, after which they are plucked and sun-dried. Because the dried bird's-eye chili pepper is not always available in regular grocery stores, I use the easy-to-find dried red chili peppers of the chili de arbol variety, found in small clear bags in the spice section or the Mexican international section of your grocery store. Sometimes these dried peppers are even found in the fresh produce section. When cooking with dried red chili peppers, I sometimes dry roast them first to release their flavors. I also sometimes tear these chili peppers before tossing them in the hot pan to expose the seeds, which releases more heat into the dish. If you leave them whole, the dish will not be as spicy. Different types of dried red chili peppers are also ground into a fine red pepper and used frequently in Indian cooking. In American grocery stores, the closest substitute is ground red pepper (cayenne). Dried red chili peppers can be stored for at least six months in an airtight jar in your pantry. Chili peppers are beneficial to good heart health and have been shown to reduce blood cholesterol levels. See also Red Pepper (page 30).

Fresh and dried red chili de arbol peppers

Carom seeds Also called "bishop's weed," these tiny brown seeds are a great natural remedy for an upset, gassy tummy. To this day, when I complain of an upset tummy, my mother will tell me to take a teaspoon full of carom seeds with water. The seeds look small and harmless, but if you bite into them, they release a peppery punch, though they are not spicy. Carom seeds can be found at Indian markets, and are more commonly known by their Hindi name, *ajwain* (also sometimes spelled *ajowan*). If you cannot find them, you can use dried thyme leaves as a substitute… it will be similar but not the exact sharp flavor of carom seeds. Carom seeds are not to be confused with caraway seeds.

Cayenne *See* Red pepper

Chapati flour (also called *atta*) is a whole-wheat flour made from finely ground and sifted whole durum wheat. It is used to make many Indian flatbreads. If you do not have chapati flour, you can substitute a mix of common whole wheat flour and all-purpose flour, and I indicate the exact amounts in the recipes. Some bags of Indian chapati flour say "100% whole wheat flour" on them, but if you compare it with American whole wheat flour, you'll notice the American one is darker. This is because Indian chapati flour is usually sifted after being milled to separate out some of the brownish coarser outer layers of the whole grain, thus making chapati flour not as nutritious as un-sifted whole wheat flour. Store chapati flour in an airtight jar in your pantry up to three months. Because chapati flour has natural oil in it, it can go rancid if kept over three months, but keeping it in the freezer can prolong the life of the flour for at least up to six months. See also All-purpose flour (page 24) and Whole wheat flour (page 31).

Cheese *See* Paneer

Cilantro *See* Coriander leaves

Cinnamon Cinnamon sticks are intensely flavored woody rolls of dried inner bark from the cinnamon tree. When using cinnamon sticks, it is important to use just a small piece because it gives a very strong flavor. You can break a cinnamon stick with your hands, but to get smaller pieces, lay the stick on a cutting board and hit it with a rolling pin to break it up. My daughter loves chewing on cinnamon sticks and it reminds me of when I was a child, I would like to take about a finger-length piece of cinnamon stick and use it as a straw to drink water for cinnamon-flavored water! Ground cinnamon is also available and may be sprinkled on top of Indian Cappuccino (page 118) as an added touch. . Cinnamon acts as a brain tonic and boosts cognitive function and memory.

Cloves have a very distinct flavor and aroma and should be used sparingly so as not to overpower a dish. A clove is a small brown woody piece with a pronged, rounded tip, which almost resembles a tiny nail. Cloves are grown on tropical evergreen clove trees, and are actually the unopened flower bud that grows in clusters. After the green buds are fully grown and just about to open, they are picked off the tree and sun dried until they become dark brown and woody. Cloves are sold whole or ground, but I prefer to buy the whole cloves so that I can dry roast and grind them when I make the Garam Masala (page 109). I also use whole cloves to flavor Vegetable Rice Pilaf (page 65). Cloves are used as a home remedy for a toothache. Pressing a clove between the jaws, at the site of the aching tooth eases the pain.

Coconut milk and shredded coconut Coconut milk is extracted from the pulp of coconuts. It is not the coconut water or "juice," the liquid inside the coconut that is clean and thin and should ideally be quite sweet. The milk, instead, is white and creamy and makes an excellent rich vegan and gluten-free base for coconut curry dishes. For fresh coconut milk, one may extract the milk themselves by pressing the white coconut meat, but canned coconut milk is available in the international sections of grocery stores. Coconut milk is fattening, although still healthy since it contains many vitamins and minerals. The fat in coconut quickly turns into energy instead of storing as fat. A light version of coconut milk is available, which I think is a suitable substitute. Unopened cans can be kept for months in your pantry—though do keep an eye on the expiration date. Shake the can thoroughly before opening since the cream may have risen to the top. Transfer any leftover coconut milk from the can into a glass or plastic container, cover it, and refrigerate it for no more than three days. Shredded coconut is the white meat that has been dried and then shredded or grated into flakes. I use dried, shredded flakes that have been sweetened when making my Chocolate and Coconut Covered Cherries (page 124). Dried, shredded coconut can be found in the baking section of a grocery store. They may be stored in an airtight container in your pantry for a few months, or until the expiration date.

Coriander leaves (also called cilantro)

Coriander leaves (also called cilantro) are used in Indian cooking both as a garnish and as an ingredient. It keeps about three days in the refrigerator before it starts discoloring and wilting. I store the bunch in a plastic bag in the refrigerator and tear off a handful or chop off a small quantity when I need to use some. Coriander leaves should be thoroughly washed before being chopped. Since there is no need to destem the leaves, you may chop the leaves and stems together. If you put some whole coriander seeds in your garden, or even in a pot indoors by a sunny window, you will soon have fresh coriander leaves always on hand. Coriander leaves are rich in cancer-fighting antioxidants.

Coriander seeds grow into the coriander plant, which gives us the fragrant coriander leaves (cilantro). The seeds have a light and sweet citrus, almost orange-like, undertone that comes out more when they are roasted. I used ground coriander and the whole seeds, both of which are available in the spice section of grocery stores. You may grind whole seeds as needed for a fresher and more intense flavor, but to make things easy, I simply use pre-ground coriander. However, if you roast whole seeds before grinding, a more intense flavor develops, which is fully released when the seeds are ground up. Whole roasted seeds are one of the main spices in my Garam

Masala page 109). Coriander seeds help fight diabetes by reducing blood sugar levels.

Cornmeal is dried corn kernels that have been finely or coarsely ground. In the United States, when cornmeal is finely ground, it is called corn flour (but in Britain, *corn flour* actually refers to *cornstarch*). Cornmeal is gluten-free and either yellow, white, or blue, depending on the type of corn used. I use the commonly found yellow cornmeal, which also has more vitamin A than the white one. Polenta is a popular Italian porridge (mush) made from cornmeal. Cornmeal can be kept in an airtight container in your pantry up to three to four months. Finely ground cornmeal is used to make delicious flatbreads such as Fenugreek Cornbreads (page 62) and Indian Cornbread (page 61). Yellow cornmeal is rich in antioxidants known to prevent cancer.

Cornstarch (referred to as *corn flour* in British recipes, although actual corn flour is a different product in the US) is a dense, powdery "flour" obtained from the endosperm (inner part) of the corn kernel. It is used as a thickening agent for sauces, puddings, and custard, such as in my Fruit Custard (page 122) recipe. Since it tends to form clumps, it is mixed with a small amount of cold liquid to form a smooth, thin paste before being stirred into a hot mixture. Cornstrach is a carbohydrate, which gives our body energy.

Cumin seeds are tiny brown-colored oval seeds that are a must-have in my pantry. Cumin flavors rice and many other dishes amazingly well. I do not cook with ground cumin; instead I prefer to use whole cumin seeds. To release their flavor, cumin seeds are often added to heated oil (temper-

ing) and incorporated directly into a dish or they are dry roasted and then ground. When they are added to heated oil, they will quickly darken. To keep the seeds from burning and turning black, you must quickly add the next ingredient. Luckily, since cumin seeds are usually introduced in the first steps of cooking a dish, if you do burn them you can just discard them along with the oil and try again. This spice provides a whole different level of flavor when it is dry roasted and crushed, and can be added to tofu marinades as well as to different types of yogurt condiments known as *raita*. Cumin seeds help your body digest food, reduce gas, and soothe indigestion.

Cream (half-and-half and heavy cream) When raw milk sits it will naturally separate into the milk fat rich cream on top and almost fat-free milk on bottom. The different types of creams are distinguished by the amount of milk fat in the mixture. Half-and-half, which I use in the Sweetened Carrots (page 123) dessert to give a rich milky base, is equal parts milk and cream and has about 10% to 12% milk fat. "Whipping cream" is a bit heavier with about 30% milk fat. I use heavy cream, also called "heavy whipping cream," to give a creamy consistency to Creamed Swiss Chard with Cheese Cubes (page 107). Heavy cream has a milk fat content of about 36% to 40% making any dish with cream taste great, but of course it should be eaten in moderation!

Edamame is the Japanese name for fresh green soybeans. These soybeans are picked before they completely mature. Edamame can be used in place of frozen or fresh green peas, thus adding protein to the dish. It may be sold as fresh pods, but is more often found in the frozen section of the grocery store and comes in pods or may be shelled. The frozen edamame pods may be steamed in the microwave and enjoyed as snack along with some salt sprinkled on top of the pods. My daughter enjoys eating edamame and has learnt how to suck out the soybeans and then discard the pod. These legumes are easy to digest and are high in fiber and protein.

Fennel seeds are small light-green seeds that come from the fennel plant. Sometimes the use and name of fennel seeds is incorrectly interchanged with anise seeds, which have a somewhat similar flavor and appearance. Fennel seeds are commonly used as a natural breath freshener when it is chewed thoroughly and then swallowed. You may notice that in many Indian restaurants, near the door, there is a bowl with fennel seeds mixed with sugar for guests to chew on after their meal. When chewed and swallowed, the fennel mixture gives fresh breath with a sweet taste and aids in digestion. You can also simply chew the fennel seeds without sugar.

Flour *See* All-purpose flour, Chapati flour, Cornmeal, Cornstarch, Gram flour, Whole wheat flour

Garam Masala (Roasted Spice Mix)
In Hindi, *garam* means "hot" and *masala* means "spices," so Garam Masala can be translated as "hot spices." In fact, this spice mixture is not as spicy as it is warming and aromatic. Garam Masala is a roasted spice mix that is commonly used in cooking throughout India. A combination of select whole spices is dry roasted and then ground to release amazing aromas. Although this spice mix is commonly available in most grocery stores, each brand will have a slightly different flavor. In general, most Garam Masala mixes will contain coriander seeds, cardamom, black peppercorns, cloves, cumin seeds, and cinnamon, but some brands of spice mixes may leave out or add certain spices, such as bay leaves, nutmeg, and black cardamoms. For convenience, you can use the pre-blended mixes available in stores, but for the best flavor I recommend you make your own homemade batch with freshly roasted and ground spices (see page 109 for a recipe).

Garlic The assertive flavor of garlic makes it one of my favorite cooking ingredients. Though mincing garlic may seem tedious, it's definitely worth it for the flavor it adds to a dish (see page 22 for instructions on working with garlic). I have found that pre-minced bottled garlic doesn't come close to the strong aroma and flavor of fresh garlic, so do try to avoid to using the pre-minced garlic. Garlic should be stored loosely covered (a paper bag is ideal) in a cool dark place away from direct sun or heat. I like to keep mine no longer than three to four weeks, but you can store it longer (just discard it when it has started to dry out). You can store the unused peeled cloves in an airtight container in the refrigerator for up to a week. Garlic is good for a healthy heart and immune system.

Ginger is a root with a unique flavor and aroma, and is a must-have in my mother's refrigerator. It is sold in the fresh produce section of grocery stores. If the root pieces are too big, you can snap off the desired size you want to buy (see page 22 for instructions on working with ginger). It keeps for two to three weeks when put in a paper bag and stored in the crisper drawer of the refrigerator. The exposed cut end of a partially used piece of ginger root should be tightly wrapped with plastic wrap before placing it back in the refrigerator. Ginger has been shown to be an effective remedy for nausea and vomiting from motion sickness.

Gram flour (called *besan* in Hindi), also known as chickpea flour, is made from a dried, spilt and skinned legume called Bengal gram. Bengal gram is a small dark brown chickpea (*kala channa*). They are different from the bigger cream-colored chickpea known as the "garbanzo." When Bengal gram is split and skinned, a yellow lentil called *channa daal* is revealed. This is crushed to make gram flour, which is pale yellow in color. You may find this gluten-free flour in the international section of grocery stores, or you may find it at an organic store. I use gram flour to make the batter for Spinach and Fenugreek Fritters (page 46) and also Opo Squash Fritters (page 51). Store gram flour in an airtight jar in your pantry for up to three months, or up to six months in your freezer.

Legumes are plants that have seed pods that split when ripe. Beans, lentils, soybeans, and peanuts are types of legumes. When the seeds of a legume are dried, they are called pulses, such as dried kidney beans, dried black-eyed peas, or dried lentils. Legumes are low in fat, a good source of carbohydrates, and rich in protein, which is essential to maintain a healthy body. They are a substitute for some of the protein in meat, which has more fat and cholesterol.

Mustard seeds (black) Mustard seeds come in two types: white and black. I use the ones that are dark brown in color, but are called "black" on the label. The white seeds are larger than and not as pungent as the darker seeds, and are used to make American mustards. Mustard seeds are used in the tempering process of cooking, in which spices are introduced to heated oil, causing the flavors to release. They are also ground and added to pickling recipes. Some people believe that mustard seeds

Lentils (whole and skinned/split)
are a type of pulse that are dried legumes. Lentils are usually dried since they last longer that way. Lentils usually have small lens-shaped seeds. Lentils are a significant part of Indian agriculture dating back from thousands of years. It is typical to see the different variety of lentils go by their Indian name, even in American markets. Lentils, called *daal* in Hindi, are used in two forms—either whole (*sabut*) or hulled (skin/shell removed) and split (*dhuli*). Sometimes lentils are split with the skin still on. When whole lentils are skinned and split, they reveal a different color and taste when cooked. Some lentils take a while to cook and, as a result, are traditionally cooked in pressure cookers. Because split lentils are thinner than whole lentils, they respond to heat better and cook faster. Lentils can be kept for six months in an airtight jar in your pantry. Be careful not to let any water in the jar, or to use wet hands or utensils to scoop lentils out of their jar. Lentils and legumes are also an excellent source of protein and folate, a vitamin that helps the body build new cells. Folate is an especially important nutrient for women who are either pregnant or planning to become pregnant.

Bengal gram (*Kala channa* and *Channa daal*) When the tiny dark brown chickpea (*kala channa*), also known as the legume "Bengal gram," is skinned and split, a bright yellow lentil is revealed, which is called *channa daal* in Hindi. This lentil is also ground into gram flour (*besan*) for use in breads and the batter to make Spinach and Fenugreek Fritters (page 46). The skinned and split Bengal gram is not the same as skinned and split yellow peas (field peas) nor is it the same as skinned and split pigeon peas (*toor daal*), although all three varieties look similar.

Red Lentils (*Masoor daal*) Whole red lentils (*sabut masoor daal*) are disc-shaped with a flat base and are reddish-tan to light brown in color. In America, whole red lentils are commonly used to make lentil soup and can readily be found in the grocery stores. The American red lentils are slightly larger and lighter in color and more tan, whereas the Indian red lentils at the ethnic markets are smaller and redder in color, but either will do fine. Spanish pardina lentils may be used in place of these whole red lentils. When whole red lentils are skinned and split, a beautiful orange color comes through and, surpris-

ingly, when they are cooked, they turn yellow. The hulled red lentils are also known as "petite crimson lentils" or *dhuli masoor daal*.

Green Lentils (*Mung daal*) Whole green lentils (*sabut mung daal*) look like tiny dark green ovals. In addition to cooking these lentils, they may also be sprouted and tossed with fresh vegetables to make a lovely Fresh Lentil Sprout Salad (page 79). When these lentils are skinned and split (*dhuli mung daal*), they reveal a yellow color, and can quickly be made into a lentil stew. The hulled green lentils are also known as "petite golden lentils."

Black gram (*Urad daal*) When whole, these tiny lentils are black and are called "black gram" or *sabut urad daal*. When they are skinned and split, they are white. The white skinned and split lentil (*dhuli urad daal*) may be roasted to add flavor to rice and other dishes.

FROM LEFT TO RIGHT: **Green lentils (*Mung daal*) (hulled and whole), Red lentils (*Masoor daal*) (hulled and whole), Black gram (*Mung daal*) (hulled and whole), Bengal gram (*Channa daal* and *Kala Channa*) (hulled and whole)**

ward off evil and negative forces, so if you feel things are not going well, try sprinkling some mustard seeds around you and the outside of your home to see if your luck changes! If anything, you might get pretty yellow mustard plants growing around your house. Black mustard seeds are an excellent source of omega-3 fatty acids which are good for healthy heart and brain function.

Nutmeg is the light brown seed of a fruit from an evergreen tree. It is best to buy it whole and grate it on the prickly side of a box grater or a microplane when ready to use to get the maximum flavor. The unused portion should be kept in your pantry in an airtight bottle. You can also simply buy a small amount of pre-ground nutmeg, but do keep in mind that ground nutmeg soon loses its flavor. Nutmeg has a flavor that is similar to but different from cinnamon. I sprinkle some nutmeg on Indian Cappuccino (page 118) as an added treat. Nutmeg is a natural sleep aid, a pinch of ground nutmeg in a cup of warm milk will relax you and induce sleep.

Oil allows food to delicately brown and also adds fat, which of course means adding flavor! Oil also prevents food from sticking to the bottom of cookware, especially if you are not using nonstick cookware. I usually cook with either vegetable oil or canola oil, which is a specific type of vegetable oil that is expressed from the seeds of the rapeseed plant and is good for deep-frying. For simplicity, I call for vegetable oil in the recipes throughout this book, but you can certainly use canola oil instead, which is healthier and lowers cholesterol. Olive oil is also a good, healthy oil to cook with, but since it is not a neutral oil, it imparts its flavor into the dish. Once opened, store oil tightly closed in a cabinet for up to six months.

Paneer is a fresh homemade Indian cheese that is un-ripened—meaning, it has not been aged. It is a mild, versatile cheese that does not melt when heated due to its chemical structure. This cheese is simply made by separating boiling milk into curds (solid clumps) and whey (watery liquid) by using lime juice. The whey is then drained by passing it through cheesecloth, leaving the moist, soft and crumbly curds, making the Indian cheese, *paneer*. Depending on what you want to make with the *paneer*, it can be used as is in its crumbled form or it may be shaped into a square and pressed under a heavy weight so the remaining whey is pressed out, leaving a firm cheese block that can be cut into pieces and fried or sautéed. I always prefer to use whole milk instead of reduced fat milk when making *paneer* so that I can get the maximum yield of *paneer* that is rich and creamy with a beautiful texture. *Paneer* is usually made from cow or buffalo milk, and should be used immediately, or kept in the refrigerator only one day so it does not dry out. *Paneer* blocks can be found in the refrigerated and frozen sections of Indian grocery stores, and even fried *paneer* cubes can be found in the frozen section. But because fresh *paneer* is so easy to make, I prefer to make it at home. Tofu may be substituted for *paneer*. *Paneer* has a good amount of calcium, which helps build strong bones and teeth and helps prevent osteoporosis.

Paprika is made from sweet peppers (usually bell peppers) that have been allowed to turn red on the plant before being plucked, set to dry, and ground. Paprika is usually not hot, and might even have a sweet taste to it, depending on the crop of the bell peppers used. I use paprika as a natural food coloring in dishes such as Tandoori Tofu Kebabs (page 113) so I like to buy the brightest red paprika I can find.

Don't be afraid to add an extra teaspoon of paprika to the dish you are cooking if you prefer a deeper color. After all, it does come from a sweet pepper, so it can't spice up your dish too much! Paprika is good for the cardiovascular systems. It is a stimulant and improves circulation and helps normalize blood pressure.

Quinoa is a nutritious gluten-free whole grain native to South America that is considered a complete protein, meaning it has all of the essential amino acids to make the proteins our body needs. This tiny bead shaped grain has a natural saponin coating, which can lend to a bitter taste. The bitter coating can be removed by thoroughly washing the quinoa and rubbing the grains with your fingertips so that the nutty flavor can come through. Quinoa cooks similarly to rice, and in fact can be substituted for many rice dishes to create even healthier dishes. I make a delicious Quinoa Cashew Pilaf (page 60) that both my daughter and husband enjoy eating. Quinoa has natural oils in it, so to keep quinoa from going rancid, I keep the grains in the refrigerator for up to three months and in the freezer for up to six months.

Red pepper (ground) (cayenne) is the generic term for several varieties of spicy hot red chilies, commonly available in red pepper flakes or the ground form. I use the ground form, which is commonly sold as ground cayenne or ground red pepper. Ground cayenne pepper is a blend of various tropical chili peppers, including the cayenne chili that have been dried and ground. It provides heat to a dish. If you feel a dish is too spicy or not spicy enough based on the amount of ground red pepper indicated in one of my recipes, you can simply add more or less to meet your personal preference. When buying ground red pepper, you may notice that they come in different heat intensities and hues of red, which is due to the batch and variety of red chili peppers from which it was made. If you happen to get any of it on your hands, be sure to thoroughly wash them so you do not touch your lips, nose, or rub your eyes and cause irritation. Cayenne is used as a natural pain killer with anti-inflammatory properties to help give relief from arthritis. *See also* Chili peppers, red (page 25).

Rice *See* Basmati rice and Brown rice

Saffron crocus flower produces saffron threads, which are the stigma of the flower. Each flower gives only three saffron threads, which must be hand-picked and dried, making this the world's most expensive spice. Luckily, only a little bit of saffron is needed when cooking, since it is potent. This exotic spice tints dishes a delicate yellow, and adds a unique complex flavor reminiscent of sweet, metallic honey. The Spanish rice dish, paella, has saffron in it, and I use saffron in my Saffron, Fruit and Nut Rice (page 66). Saffron has also been used to dye cloth a deep yellow, and also in perfumery and to make medicines. A pinch of saffron stirred in with milk before bed helps in sleep disorders like insomnia. Saffron also improves eye and vision health. Saffron may be stored in an airtight container placed in a cool, dry place such as your pantry for up to six months.

Tamarind concentrate (paste)
Tamarind, called *imlee* in Hindi, is a fruit pod of the tamarind tree that grows around the world, though it is especially abundant in Asia. When the ripe pods are plucked from the trees, they have a thin, tan-colored shell. When the pod is opened, there is fruit pulp and seeds held together by the fibrous husk. The reddish-brown pulp is what is used in cooking, while the pod, fibers and seeds are discarded. Tamarind provides a sour tinge to food. The easiest way to use tamarind is to use pre-extracted tamarind pulp, which is also called "tamarind concentrate," "tamarind paste," or "tamarind extract." It is thick and pasty and usually can be found at natural food stores and at ethnic markets. The older the extracted pulp, the darker it turns, until it is eventually black. Because tamarind has natural preservative properties, it will keep for up to one year in your pantry. When the concentrate is heated, it thins out. Fresh ripe tamarind pods are also plucked, shelled, and then pressed into square blocks. Even though the pressed pods have not been dried, they may seem dried out depending on their age. To extract the pulp, pull of the desired amount from the block and soak it is warm water until soft, about 15 minutes. Then strain it through a sieve to separate the seeds and fibrous husk. You are left with the usable pulp. You may even buy fresh whole tamarind pods and extract the pulp (concentrate) in a similar way after shelling it. Extracting the pulp from tamarind blocks or whole pods can be a messy and tedious process, that's why I prefer to buy the tamarind concentrate. Tamarind pulp is used in traditional medicines as a natural laxative. It also helps the body digest food.

Tofu is also known as soybean curd or bean curd. It is a complete plant-based protein with nine essential amino acids the body needs to maintain muscle, bone, and organs. Tofu is made from curdled soymilk, which is the iron-rich liquid extracted from cooked soybeans. After the milk is curdled with a coagulant such as calcium sulfate or lemon juice, it is separated into curds and whey and drained through a cheesecloth, similar to the cheese making process of the Indian cheese, *paneer*. The firmness (extra-firm, firm, or soft) of the tofu depends on how much whey has been extracted. Silken tofu has a smooth texture and is not as common as regular tofu. Instead of curdling the milk and separating it, silken tofu is made from soymilk that has Epsom salt added to give the milk a silky texture. Silken tofu is used in smoothies, custards, and as a spread. Regular tofu usually comes in 14 to 16 ounce (400 g to 500 g) blocks. If you are using half a block of tofu, you may store the unused portion submerged in cold water in a covered bowl in the refrigerator for up to two days. Tofu may be frozen for up to three months, but upon thawing, the texture changes, making it slightly chewier. Since tofu does not have much flavor itself, it takes on the flavor of the food with which it is cooked. The Indian cheese *paneer* may be substituted for Tofu. Tofu is easy to digest, low in calories and sodium, cholesterol free, and a good source of iron, which is needed for oxygen transport in our body.

Turmeric, ground is a beautiful bright yellow spice made from the turmeric root, which is dried and ground into a powder. Turmeric root grows best in a tropical climate, making India a top producer, consumer, and exporter of this spice. This spice imparts both color and a mild earthy flavor to a dish, but if you use too much it can lend a bitter taste to the dish. Turmeric has anti-inflammatory properties and soothes inflammation and pain from arthritis. Turmeric is available at the spice aisle of grocery stores.

White rice *See* Basmati rice

Whole wheat flour is a brown, fuller flavored flour milled from the entire wheat grain (kernel), thus called whole wheat flour. The whole grain includes the bran (the outer coating), germ (the sprouting part), and endosperm (inner part), meaning the milled flour has high fiber, vitamin, and mineral content. Breads made from whole grains or whole wheat flour are compared to white breads, which are made from refined grains.

Chapter 1

Pickles and Chutneys

An Indian meal usually has a basic accompaniment, such as plain yogurt or spiced yogurt (*raita*), pickled fruit or vegetable, or a chutney. *Raita* is plain yogurt that has been whisked until smooth and a few spices and vegetables are added to it. Soy yogurt may be used to make a vegan *raita*.

Pickled fruits and vegetables (*achar*) are another condiment typically offered with Indian meals. Pickling preserves food in salt, oil, or vinegar and can taste tart, tangy, slightly bitter, and spicy. *Achar* is commonly made with ginger or fruits, such as lemons, limes, or mangoes; or vegetables such as carrots and beets. One of my favorite pickles is the sweet and tangy Pickled Carrots, Turnips, and Cauliflower (page 34).

You may have heard the word chutney, which is now a commonly used word. Chutney is the Hindi word for a relish that is made either from crushed herbs or mashed fruits with added spices. Chutneys can be spicy, sweet, sour, or have a combination of these taste components. You can use chutneys as a dipping sauce or as a jam. Opo Squash Fritters (page 57) and Tandoori Tofu Kebabs (page 113) can be dipped in Fresh Coriander Chutney (page 37). Sweet and Spicy Pear Chutney (page 36) can be spread on bread, toast, English muffins, or bagels. Here, we will make an assortment of chutneys from peanuts, pears, and fresh coriander leaves.

Spiced Yogurt with Potatoes

Like my mother and most Indians, I always have plain yogurt in my refrigerator, which is usually homemade. Yogurt is typically eaten along with meals as a cooling condiment that soothes your stomach from spicy foods. To jazz up plain yogurt, it is common to whisk in different vegetables and just a wee bit of spices to make a *raita*. My favorite *raita* has always been this one my mom makes with boiled potatoes. My baby loves for me to put this *raita* in a small bowl for her, which I don't mind because it is an excellent source of dairy and good for her growing bones.

Serves 4 to 6
Prep time: 10 minutes
Refrigerator Life: 3 hours (tastes best when freshly made)

1 medium russet potato (about ½ lb/225 g), boiled (see page 20)
1 cup (250 g) plain yogurt or plain soy yogurt (regular or fat free)
¼ cup (65 ml) water
¼ teaspoon cumin seeds, roasted and ground (see page 24)
2 pinches ground red pepper (cayenne)
¼ heaping teaspoon salt
¼ teaspoon ground black pepper

1 Peel the boiled potato and dice into ¼-inch (6 mm) cubes.
2 Whisk the yogurt in a large bowl until it is smooth
3 Add the water, cumin, red pepper, salt, and black pepper. Mix well.
4 Add the potato cubes. Mix together. Enjoy now or refrigerate for later. Serve chilled.

Avocado and Coriander
Spiced Yogurt

Tomato, Cucumber, and
Onion Spiced Yogurt

Spiced Yogurt with Potatoes

Variation 1

Avocado and Coriander Spiced Yogurt

With a major Mexican influence here in Texas, especially with the cuisine, avocados and coriander (also called cilantro) are very popular, so I thought of making a *raita* out of them. When ripe, avocados will yield slightly to the touch instead of being hard. Avocados, which are categorized as a fruit, help reduce the signs of aging, regulate blood sugar level, and promote eye health.

Follow steps 2 through 4 for Spiced Yogurt with Potatoes (page 32), but in step 4, do not add the potato. Instead, add one avocado, diced into ¼-inch (6 mm) cubes, juice of ½ lime and 1 handful fresh coriander leaves (about ¼ cup/10 g packed leaves), rinsed and finely chopped.

Dicing an Avocado
1 Using a small knife, cut the avocado in half lengthwise around the pit.

2 Hold the avocado in both hands and twist the halves in opposite directions to separate them.
3 Scoop out the pit with a spoon. If it is hard to remove, carefully stab the pit with a knife. Pull out the knife with the pit and discard.
4 Using a spoon, scoop out the avocado flesh from the skin. It should come away from the skin easily in one part.
5 Dice each avocado half into about ¼-inch (6 mm) cubes.

Variation 2

Tomato, Cucumber, and Onion Spiced Yogurt

My hubby's favorite *raita* has tomatoes, cucumber and onions in it. You may use any variety of cucumber such as an English or Japanese cucumber. The high water content, vitamins A, B & C and the presence of certain minerals like magnesium, potassium, and silica make cucumbers an essential part of skin care, such as putting sliced cucumbers on one's eyes to reduce puffiness.

Follow steps 2 through 4 for Spiced Yogurt with Potatoes (page 32), but in step 4, do not add the potato. Instead, add 2 tablespoons minced onion; 1 small tomato, such as a plum (Roma), finely diced, and 4 tablespoons peeled and finely diced cucumber (any variety).

Pickled Carrots, Turnips, and Cauliflower

There are so many varieties of pickled fruit and vegetables in India, called *achar* in Hindi. They are served as a condiment along with a meal for a crunch between bites. My favorite *achar* is this mixed vegetable pickle made from carrots, turnips, and cauliflower. My mom makes this pickle once every summer to enjoy over the entire year, as it takes a handful of spices to make.

Make 2 lbs (1 kg) pickle
Prep time: 25 minutes + 30 minutes sitting + 7 days sitting
Cook time: 15 minutes to bring water to a boil
Shelf Life: 1 year

Pickled Beets

Pickled Carrots

Pickled Carrots, Turnips, and Cauliflower

2 cups (225 g) baby carrots or 5 medium carrots
4 small turnips (total 1 lb/500 g)
2¼ cups (225 g) fresh bite-size cauliflower florets or ½ small head fresh cauliflower cut into florets (see page 24)
8 cups (1.75 liters) water
1½ cups (200 g) light brown sugar
1 cup (250 ml) mustard oil
1 cup (250 ml) vinegar
3 tablespoons plus 1 teaspoon salt
10 tablespoons coarsely ground mustard seeds
2 tablespoons ground cinnamon
2 teaspoons ground cloves
2 tablespoons ground cumin seeds
2 tablespoons ground red pepper (cayenne)
2 tablespoons ground black pepper
½ cup (100 g) peeled and finely grated fresh ginger

1 Wash the baby carrots. Cut each baby carrot into half lengthwise. If using whole carrots, peel and cut into thick matchsticks (see page 23)
2 Wash the turnips. Cut off the tops and discard. Peel each turnip. Cut each turnip into four segments. Cut each segment into slices about ¼ inch (6 mm) thick.
3 Pour the water into a medium-sized stockpot. Bring to a rolling boil over high heat, which takes about 15 minutes. Immerse the turnips, carrots, and cauliflower into the boiling water. Immediately pour out the vegetables into a colander in the sink and drain the water.
4 Line a baking sheet with a kitchen towel. Spread the vegetables out on the towel. Place a paper towel over the vegetables and place in the sunlight for 30 minutes to dry. (Excess moisture on the vegetables can cause them to turn moldy.)
5 Place the remaining ingredients in a large bowl and mix together. Add the vegetables pieces and mix well.
6 Pour the vegetables and any liquid into a large glass or plastic jar. Put the lid on the jar and shake it so everything is mixed well. Place the closed jar by a sunny windowsill for a week so the flavors will develop, shaking the jar once a day.
7 Enjoy a few pieces of the pickle along with a meal, and store the rest in the jar in your pantry or cabinet at room temperature for up to 1 year! The oil will settle at the bottom of the jar, so shake or stir before serving.

Pickled Carrots

An Indian hole-in-the-wall cafe that we have been frequenting since I was a child has a tangy pickled carrot they offer as a condiment that has a nice bite to it. It is quite similar to these Pickled Carrots that have a unique flavor from coarsely ground mustard seeds. Carrots without their leafy tops will stay fresh for about one week stored in a plastic bag in the refrigerator's vegetable drawer. Avoid carrots that have splits or cracks, or that are limp. Carrots have vitamin A, which is good for your eyes and clear, healthy skin. Enjoy a few bites of this crunchy carrot pickle along with your meal.

Make 2 cups (225 grams)
Prep time: 10 minutes + 2 days sitting
Refrigerator Life: 2 weeks

5 medium carrots, peeled and cut into thick matchsticks (see page 23)
1½ teaspoons coarsely ground black/brown mustard seeds
½ teaspoon ground turmeric
½ teaspoon ground red pepper (cayenne)
1½ teaspoons salt
2 tablespoons lime juice
1 tablespoon vegetable oil
1 fresh finger-length green chili pepper, cut lengthwise into thin slices (any variety)

1 Pat the carrot pieces with a kitchen towel to make sure there is no excess water that can cause the pickle to turn moldy.
2 Place the rest of the ingredients (except the green pepper) in a glass or plastic jar. Mix to combine.
3 Add the carrots and sliced green chili pepper. Put the lid on the jar and shake it so everything is mixed well. Place the closed jar by a sunny windowsill for 2 days so the flavors will develop. Shake the jar once a day.
4 Enjoy a few pieces of the pickle along with a meal and refrigerate the rest in a jar for up to 2 weeks.

Pickled Beets

Beets, also known as beetroot (*chukandar* in Hindi), are a root vegetable that make a crunchy pickle. Beets are very staining, and you might find your hands colored purple, so be sure to immediately wash your hands after working with them. Choose firm beets that are small to medium in size since they will be more tender than larger ones. Remove any leafy tops since they draw moisture from the bulb, and then store in a plastic bag in the refrigerator for up to one week. Beets stimulate our bodies to produce serotonin, a natural compound that contributes to feelings of happiness and well-being.

Make ½ lb pickled beets (225 grams)
Prep time: 10 minutes + 10 days sitting
Refrigerator Life: 2 weeks

1 beet (about ½ lb/225 g)
1 teaspoon coarsely ground black/brown mustard seeds
¼ teaspoon ground red pepper (cayenne)
¾ teaspoon salt
¼ teaspoon ground black pepper
1 tablespoon vegetable oil
3 tablespoons vinegar

1 Cut off both ends of the beet and discard. Peel the beat. Rinse the beet with cold water and pat dry with a paper towel. Cut the beet in half lengthwise. Slice each half into thin semi-circles, about ¼ inch (6 mm) thick. Wash your hands so they will not be purple.
2 Place the rest of the ingredients in a glass or plastic jar. Mix to combine.
3 Add the beets. Put the lid on the jar and shake it so everything is mixed well. Place the closed jar by a sunny windowsill for 10 days so the flavors will develop. Shake the jar once a day. The beets will have a bit of crunch to them.
4 Enjoy a few pieces of the pickle along with a meal or in a salad and refrigerate the rest in a jar for up to 2 weeks.

Roasted Peanut Chutney

The aroma of freshly made peanut chutney from roasted peanuts with a bit of spicy kick might have you packing PB&J sandwiches for yourself to take to work! My mother-in-law makes this chutney to enjoy along with steamed rice cakes (*idli*) and rice and lentil crêpes (*dosa*). Peanuts are rich calcium which is good for healthy bones. They also have protein, which is good for muscle development. Shelled peanuts may be refrigerated for up to a year. Peanuts with their skins on have cancer-fighting antioxidants.

Makes 1¼ cups (280 g)
Prep time: 5 minutes
Cook time: 2 minutes
Refrigerator Life: 7 days
Reheating method: None! Stir the refrigerated chutney and serve either chilled or at room temperature.

1 cup (145 g) plain shelled peanuts, with skins on (not roasted or salted)
3 dried finger-length red chili peppers
2 teaspoons tamarind concentrate (black paste)
1 large clove garlic
¾ teaspoon salt
1 cup (250 ml) plus 1 tablespoon water

1 Place a medium skillet over medium-high heat. When the skillet is heated, add the peanuts and roast them until the skins start to get dark brown spots on them, stirring frequently, about 2 minutes. Push the roasted peanuts to one side of the skillet and turn off the heat.
2 Add the red chili peppers to the hot skillet and roast them until they slightly puff up and start turning a blackish color, stirring frequently, about 2 minutes.
3 Place the roasted peanuts, roasted red chili peppers, tamarind, garlic, salt, and water in a blender and process until smooth and spreadable. Do not fully purée it. Enjoy now or refrigerate for later!

ABOUT CELERY The leaves may be cut off to use for salads, and the stalks (also called ribs) may be enjoyed raw, in soups, or along with my roasted peanut chutney to spread on top. Choose tightly formed bunches with crisp green leaves. You may refrigerate them in a plastic bag for up to one week. Celery is known to reduce blood pressure.
DIRECTIONS ON HOW TO CUT CELERY INTO STICKS If buying a whole bunch of celery, cut off the root end and discard. Cut off the leaves and the top end at discard. Wash the stalks. Cut the stalks crosswise into 3 even pieces. Cut each celery piece lengthwise into 3 to 4 sticks.

Sweet and Spicy Pear Chutney

Start your morning off with a sweet and spicy pear chutney to spread as a jam on toast. I also enjoy pear chutney on white bread for a light sandwich. Choose pears that yield slightly to the touch and have a sweet fragrance. Pears relieve asthma symptoms, help prevent high blood pressure and stroke and have antioxidants that may help protect women against postmenopausal breast cancer.

Makes ¼ cup (75 g)
Prep time: 10 minutes + overnight sitting
Cook time: 20 minutes
Refrigerator Life: 1 month
Reheating method: None! Spread and serve!

3 small ripe pears (any variety) (total 1 lb/500 g)
4 tablespoons sugar
¼ teaspoon ground red pepper (cayenne)
¼ teaspoon salt

1 Wash and peel the pears. Grate the pears on the small grating holes of a box grater. Discard the seeds. The grated pears will be soft, mushy, and watery.
2 Place the grated pears (and any liquid from the pears) and sugar in a medium bowl. Mix well. Cover and let sit for 12 hours at room temperature.
3 Place the grated pear and sugar mixture, red pepper, and salt in a small saucepan over medium heat. Stir to combine. Simmer until the chutney becomes sticky and you no longer see any liquid in the saucepan, stirring frequently, about 18 to 20 minutes. The chutney will turn a beautiful golden orange color with a glisten and will also clump together when you stir it. It should cook down to about ¼ cup (75 g). Turn off the heat. The chutney will have the consistency of a very soft spreadable jam.
4 Let cool to room temperature and then refrigerate. The chutney will thicken to a jam as it chills. Enjoy!

Sweet and Spicy Pear
Chutney

Fresh Coriander
Chutney

Roasted Peanut
Chutney

Fresh Coriander Chutney

Fresh coriander leaves (cilantro) make an easy, versatile chutney. This chutney can be used as a spread in sandwiches, or can be served with Tandoori Tofu Kebabs (page 113) for dipping. Look for bunches with bright green leaves with no signs of wilting. Coriander leaves may be stored up to about 3 days in a plastic bag in a refrigerator. These leaves offer relief from stomach indigestion, reduce nausea, and have antioxidant properties.

Makes 1 cup (200 g)
Prep time: 5 minutes
Refrigerator Life: 5 days
Freezer Life: 1 month
Reheating method: None. Stir the refrigerated or defrosted chutney and served either chilled or at room temperature.

1 small onion, coarsely chopped
1½ cups (60 g) packed fresh coriander leaves (cilantro), rinsed and chopped
Juice of 1 lime
¼ teaspoon ground red pepper (cayenne)
½ teaspoon salt
¼ teaspoon ground black pepper
¾ teaspoon sugar

1 Rinse the chopped onion with cold water to reduce the bitterness.
2 Process all the ingredients in a mini food processor until almost smooth, but do not purée it because some texture looks nice.
3 Enjoy now or refrigerate or freeze for later! If the chutney is bitter, refrigerate for one day to reduce the bitterness.

CHAPTER 2

Appetizers and Snacks

Fruits, nuts, and vegetables are great for healthy snacking or
to serve as appetizers when entertaining. Instead of munching on
just a plain apple, you can chop up a few of your favorite fruits
and toss with red pepper (cayenne), salt, black pepper, and a
splash of fresh lime juice to create a tangy Spiced Fruit Cocktail
(page 40). If you have too many tomatoes growing in your garden,
you can boil them to make a soothing Tomato Soup (page 47). Brussels sprouts and asparagus spears can be spiced with roasted and
ground cumin seeds to create a healthy snack, or be served as
an appetizer. You may also grill vegetables such as mushrooms,
zucchini, tomatoes, and onions on an indoor grill and toss with
a pinch of ground red pepper (cayenne) to create a beautiful
Grilled Vegetable Platter (page 42).

Vegetables, such as opo squash, and fresh greens, such as spinach and fenugreek, can be chopped up and mixed with a batter of
chickpea flour and water and then briefly fried to create delicious fritters. Nuts, such as cashews, taste wonderful when quickly deep fried and tossed with salt. Salted Fried Cashews (page 43)
pair wonderfully with an afternoon cup of Chai Tea (page 119) or
Indian Cappuccino (page 118).

Spiced Fruit Cocktail

When my mom has dinner parties, she usually makes this bright, beautiful fruit salad (fruit *chaat*) to offer as an appetizer. In India, fruit is often enjoyed with a few spices and lime juice that gives a spicy, tangy twist to sweet fruits. When in season, guavas are the highlight of this fruit salad, and are an unexpected flavorful treat when people bite into them. I have included my favorite fruits in this recipe, but you may choose your desired fruits. Do remember that bananas are an Indian favorite! The acidity of the lime juice delays browning, so you can prepare this dish up to an hour in advance before serving. This colorful fruit salad is full of health benefits because fruit is low in fat and calories, and a good source of fiber.

ABOUT GUAVA Guava, or *amrood* in Hindi, is a sweet, tropical round fruit that has an amazing fragrance and robust flavor. It has a thin yellowish to light green skin, similar to a pear, with flesh that ranges in color from creamish white to beautiful bright pink. To eat a guava, rinse it first, and then either cut it in cubes, or just bite into it, keeping the skin on. Be careful when eating the seeds, since they can be hard. You could also cut around the middle seeded area. Guavas are in season in the summer months. Look for ones that are slightly tender to the touch, and not too hard. Guava can be stored in the refrigerator up to one week, but you might not want to keep it that long, since the strong aroma permeates the refrigerator, and into the freezer and ice cubes, and your entire house! Guavas are rich in B vitamins, which are good for healthy brain and nerve function.

Other fruits that you may substitute:
Peach, Asian pear, strawberries, apricots, blackberries, blueberries, kiwi

Serves 6
Prep time: 10 minutes
Refrigerator life: 1 hour (Tastes best freshly tossed and served.)
Reheating method: None! Simply toss and serve.

2 guavas, chopped into bite-size cubes (peel on)
1 red apple, chopped into bite-size cubes (peel on)
1 pear, chopped into bite-size cubes (peel on)
1 plum, chopped into bite-size cubes (peel on)
1 cup (150 g) green grapes
1 banana (peeled)
¼ teaspoon ground red pepper (cayenne)
½ teaspoon salt
¼ teaspoon ground black pepper
Juice of 1 lime
Pomegranate seeds (from 1 small pomegranate), for garnish (optional)

1 Place the guava, apple, pear, plum, and grapes in a large serving bowl.
2 Cut the banana into ¼-inch (6 mm) slices and place in the bowl.
3 Add the red pepper, salt, black pepper, and lime juice. Mix well.
4 Sprinkle 2 tablespoons of the pomegranate seeds over the fruit salad. Enjoy now or refrigerate for later!

TIP: Look for pomegranates that are heavy for their size and have bright and blemish-free skin. Pomegranates are packed with antioxidants that help with making healthier and smoother skin. Pomegranate seeds stain so work with the pomegranate immersed in water to reduce staining splashes.

Fresh Exotic Fruits *Papaya, Lychees, and Loquats*

Papaya is a tropical fruit that is popular in India. It has a peculiar aroma and texture, but when tossed with spices and lime juice, it is enjoyable. Depending on the variety, the skin ranges from greenish-yellow to golden-orange. The flesh is golden orange to salmon-red color and very soft, juicy, and silky. When you cut open a papaya, you will see shiny round black seeds. When ripe, papaya will slightly yield to pressure. Store unripe papayas at room temperature for a few days until they soften and are ready to eat. You may refrigerate ripe papayas for up to three days. Papaya are good sources of vitamins A and C, which are bother needed for a healthy immune system so we can prevent getting the cold or flu.

Serves 4
Prep time: 5 minutes
Cook time: 25 minutes
Refrigerator life: 1 hour (Tastes best freshly tossed and served.)

1 papaya
½ teaspoon salt
¼ teaspoon ground black pepper
Juice of 2 limes

1 Wash and peel the papaya with a vegetable peeler. Cut off both ends and discard. Cut the papaya in half lengthwise. Using a spoon, scoop out the seeds and discard.
2 Cut each half lengthwise down the middle. Cut each segment crosswise into about 1-inch (2.5 cm) pieces
3 Place the papaya pieces in a shallow bowl. Add the salt, black pepper, and lime juice. Mix well and serve.

FRESH LYCHEES Lychees might be intimidating to eat, but are actually a fun and delicious fruit that can help relieve an annoying cough, fight acne, nourish and refine your skin. On our trips to India as a child, I remember seeing a bunch of fresh lychees on my grandmother's dining table in her veranda. All you have to do is pick a lychee off the bunch and use your fingers to peel the thick red skin off. It's easy if you start at the stem end and pry the skin away from there. Inside there will be white fleshy fruit that you can eat. There will be a black pit inside there that you'll discard. Enjoy!

FRESH LOQUATS Loquat plants are very popular in India and China, but are often grown as ornamental trees in the United States. In the spring, I see fruit filled loquat trees all around my neighborhood. I often wonder if the owners know they can actually enjoy eating the fruit, since there are so many yellow loquat clusters pulling down the branches. The fruit has a thin edible yellow skin, with pale yellow flesh inside surrounding two to four oval seeds. You can pop a whole loquat in your mouth, and the discard the seeds. Loquats have anti-cancer fighting properties and are a good source of vitamin A, which is good for healthy eyes.

Grilled Vegetable Platter

Grilling vegetables with a few spices brings out amazing flavor in them. These vegetables may be eaten as a snack, served as a side item, and even mixed in a pasta, or placed on a pizza before it goes into the oven. I especially enjoy grilled mushrooms and find it hard to stop eating them! Vegetables are low in fat and calories, and good sources of fiber, vitamins, and minerals.

Serves 4 to 6
Prep time: 10 minutes
Cook time: 25 minutes
Refrigerator life: Not recommended. (Tastes best freshly cooked and warm.)

½ lb (225 g) fresh whole or pre-sliced mushrooms
2 small zucchini (total ½ lb/225 g)
1 small red onion, cut into 8 wedges and layers separated
2 small fully ripe tomatoes, such as plum (Roma)
4 tablespoons vegetable oil
1 teaspoon ground red pepper (cayenne)
1 teaspoon salt
1 teaspoon ground black pepper

1 If you are using whole mushrooms, clean them by placing them in a colander and running cold water over them while using your fingers to gently rub away any dirt. Cut the cleaned mushrooms into ¼-inch (6 mm) or thinner longitudinal slices.

2 Wash the zucchini. Cut off both ends and discard. Do not peel the zucchini. Slice into thin circles, about ¼ inch (6 mm) thick.

3 Wash the tomatoes. Slice them into thin circles, about ¼ inch (6 mm) thick.

4 Spread 2 tablespoons of the oil into a

large nonstick skillet and place over medium heat. When the oil is heated, add the sliced mushrooms. Spread them out in a single layer. Let cook for 5 minutes, while they will start to reduce in volume as they release their water.

5 Turn the mushrooms over. Evenly sprinkle ¼ teaspoon each of the red pepper, salt, and black pepper on them. Cook until the mushrooms turn brown, gently stirring occasionally, about 6 minutes. Remove the mushrooms from the skillet and place on a serving platter.

6 Spread another 1 tablespoon of the oil on the hot skillet. Add the zucchini circles, spreading them out in a single layer. Cook for 3 minutes.

7 Turn over the zucchini. It should be brownish on the flipped side. Evenly sprinkle on ¼ teaspoon each of the red pepper, salt, and black pepper. Cook until the zucchini becomes tender, about 3 minutes. Remove the zucchini from the skillet and place on a serving platter.

8 Spread another 2 teaspoons of the oil on the hot skillet. Add the onion pieces. Evenly sprinkle on ¼ teaspoon each of the red pepper, salt, and black pepper. Cook until the onion becomes tender, but still has a bit of crisp to it, stirring occasionally, about 3 minutes. Transfer the onion from the skillet to a serving platter.

9 Spread the remaining 1 teaspoon of the oil on the hot skillet. Add the tomato circles, spreading them out in a single layer. Cook for 1 minute.

10 Turn over the tomato circles. Evenly sprinkle on the remaining ¼ teaspoon each of the red pepper, salt, and black pepper. Cook until the tomato becomes tender, about 3 minutes. Remove the tomato from the skillet and place on a serving platter.

Salted Fried Cashews

Fried and salted cashews are an addictive afternoon snack that goes great with a cup of Indian Cappuccino (page 118) or Chai Tea (page 119). They taste great freshly fried, or you can put them in an airtight container to enjoy later. These cashews are also excellent with cocktails! Cashews may be stored in the refrigerator for up to 3 months or may be frozen for up to a year. Cashews are rich in magnesium, which is good for healthy bones.

Makes 1 lb (500 g)
Cook time: 5 minutes
Shelf life: Store up to 1 month in an airtight container at room temperature.

Canola oil, for deep frying
1 lb (500 g) plain (raw) whole cashews
2 teaspoons salt

1 Pour 2 inches (5 cm) of oil into a medium wok and place over medium-high heat.

2 Test the oil to make sure it is hot by dropping 1 cashew into the wok. If the oil is bubbling around the cashew, the oil is hot and ready. If not, let the oil heat longer. If the cashew turns dark brown immediately, the oil is too hot, so reduce the heat a bit.

3 When the oil is hot and ready, reduce the heat to medium so the cashews do not burn while they are cooking. Using a spider, place a batch of cashews in the spider and lower it into the oil. Leave the spider in the wok and cook until the cashews are light golden, while using a small spoon to frequently turn the cashews in the spider, about 30 to 45 seconds. (If you do not have a spider, using a large spoon, carefully slide the cashews in batches into the wok, depending on the size of your wok and turn frequently.)

4 Remove the cashews from the wok by lifting up the spider (or with a slotted spoon) and place them in a wide bowl lined with paper towels. Immediately sprinkle the salt on the hot cashews and toss well.

5 Allow to cool slightly before serving. Enjoy now or let cool completely and store in a sealed jar at room temperature for later!

TIP: For 1 lb (500 g) of cashews, I fry them in 5 batches. Keep a very sharp eye on the first batch, as it may take less time since the oil will be very hot.

Pan-Seared Brussels Sprouts

Brussels sprouts look and taste like tiny cabbages. Searing them with garlic and roasted ground cumin seeds is a delicious way to get folates, into your diet.

Serves 3 to 4
Prep time: 5 minutes
Cook time: 15 minutes
Refrigerator life: Not recommended. (Tastes best freshly made.)

8 Brussels sprouts
1 tablespoon minced garlic
5 tablespoons vegetable oil
½ teaspoon cumin seeds, roasted and ground (see page 20)
½ teaspoon salt
¼ teaspoon ground black pepper

1 Peel off the outer layer of the Brussels sprouts and discard. Cut off the stems and discard. Wash the Brussels sprouts and pat dry with a kitchen towel. Cut each Brussels sprout in half.
2 Put the garlic and 4 tablespoons of the oil in a small bowl and microwave for 50 seconds to infuse the oil with the garlic.
3 Add the remaining 1 tablespoon of the oil to a large skillet and place over medium heat.
4 Dip each Brussels sprout half into the garlic and oil mixture and place in the skillet, flat side down. Spread out any remaining garlic on the Brussels sprouts. Evenly sprinkle on the cumin and ¼ teaspoon of the salt. Cover the skillet and cook for 5 minutes.
5 Turn the Brussels sprouts. They will be brownish and slightly crusted on the flat side. Evenly sprinkle on the black pepper and the remaining ¼ teaspoon of the salt. Cover the skillet and cook for 5 minutes, or until the Brussels sprouts are tender and you can easily insert a knife through them. Turn off the heat. Enjoy!

Oven-Roasted Asparagus Spears

When we go to a deli, my daughter insists on getting the aspargus spears she sees there. Roasted ground cumin seeds and garlic lend amazing flavor to this asparagus recipe that's healthy too!

Serves 3 to 4
Prep time: 5 minutes
Cook time: 10 minutes
Refrigerator life: Not recommended. (Tastes best freshly made.)

½ lb (225 g) asparagus spears
2 teaspoons minced garlic
1 tablespoon plus 2 teaspoons vegetable oil
½ teaspoon cumin seeds, roasted and ground (see page 20)
¼ teaspoon salt
¼ teaspoon ground black pepper
2 tablespoons blanched and slivered almonds (page 21)

1 Preheat the oven to 400°F (200°C) (a small toaster oven is more energy and time efficient).
2 Snap or cut off the woody end (the last 1 inch/2.5 cm) of the asparagus spears and discard. Wash the spears and pat dry with a kitchen towel.
3 Put the garlic and the oil in a small bowl and microwave for 50 seconds to infuse the oil with the garlic.
4 Place the asparagus spears flat on a baking sheet. Evenly drizzle the garlic and oil mixture over the spears.
5 Evenly sprinkle on the cumin, salt, and black pepper. When the oven is heated, roast the asparagus for 10 minutes. They will be bright green and tender, but still a bit crisp. You should be able to easily cut it with a knife, and not be soggy or stringy.
6 Place the spears on a platter. Evenly sprinkle the almonds on top. Enjoy!

Indian-Style Grilled Corn

In my childhood summer visits to India, we would often treat ourselves to roasted corn on the cob sold on the streets. My dad likes to make a similar version at home by grilling it and giving it a splash of lime juice and salt. Corn is a good source of fiber and has folic acid.

Serves 4
Prep time: 5 minutes
Cook time: 20 minutes
Refrigerator life: Not recommended. (Tastes best freshly grilled and served.)

4 fresh ears of corn
Juice of 1 lime
½ teaspoon salt

1 Using your hands, peel off the husks and break off the stem from the corn and discard.
2 Spray the rack of a gas grill with cooking oil. Heat up the grill on medium heat.
3 When the grill is heated, place the corn ears directly on the rack. Cook for about 20 minutes, or until the kernels are tender, turning the corn every 5 minutes or so. The corn will get some blackish marks on it.
4 When they are done, remove from the grill and place on a plate. Evenly sprinkle on the lime juice and salt on all the corn ears. Enjoy!

Variation
Quick Buttered Corn on the Cob

My dad loves to make corn in the microwave, and we all love to eat it, including our two family dogs! It tastes like boiled corn, yet it is amazingly quick to make, so you save time and energy instead of boiling them on the stovetop.

1. Working with 2 ears of corn, peel off the husks and discard. You may leave the stem on. Wrap the corn ears together in a kitchen towel and place them in the microwave for 6 minutes, turning halfway between.
2. To see if they are done, slightly unfold the towel and see if the kernels are tender by poking a knife in it. It not, continue cooking them in the microwave in 1 minute intervals, checking to see if they are done after each additional minute.
3. When they are done, remove from the microwave, unwrap the corn ears, and place on a plate. Lightly rub a stick of unsalted butter (or vegan buttery spread) around the corn ears until they have butter all around them. Evenly sprinkle on the juice of ½ lime and ¼ teaspoon of salt on the corn ears. Enjoy!

Spinach and Fenugreek Fritters

Fresh fenugreek or spinach leaves are chopped, battered, and fried to make yummy Indian vegetable fritters called *pakora*. Both fenugreek and spinach are high in vitamin K, which is good for healthy bones. These fritters make a great afternoon snack along with a cup of Chai Tea (page 119).

Serves 4 to 5
Prep time: 15 minutes + 25 minutes resting
Cook time: about 15 minutes to fry all of the fritters
Refrigerator life: Not recommended. (Tastes best freshly fried and served hot.)

½ lb (225 g) fresh spinach (1 bunch) or baby spinach
½ lb (225 g) fresh fenugreek (1 bunch)
1¾ cups (210 g) gram flour
1 fresh finger-length green chili pepper, finely chopped (any variety)
½ teaspoon ground red pepper (cayenne)
1½ teaspoons salt
½ teaspoon ground black pepper
¾ cup (185 ml) water
Canola oil, for deep-frying

1 Cut off the stems at the bottom of the spinach bunch where the leafy part ends and discard. Thoroughly wash the spinach. Finely chop the leaves. You should get about 3 cups (150 g) packed leaves. If using baby spinach, you do not need to trim the stems but do chop the leaves.
2 Cut off the stems at the bottom of the fenugreek bunch where the leafy part ends and discard. Thoroughly wash the fenugreek. Finely chop the leaves and remaining stems. You should get 2 cups (130 g) packed leaves.
3 Place all of the chopped spinach and fenugreek leaves into a colander and toss.
4 To make the batter, place the flour, green chili pepper, red pepper, salt, black pepper, and water in a medium bowl. Mix with a spoon to combine, and then beat it vigorously for 2 minutes until smooth. Set aside to rest for 15 minutes.
5 Squeeze the spinach and fenugreek to remove any excess water. Add to the batter. Using one hand, mix to combine. Set aside to rest for 10 minutes.
6 Pour 2 inches (5 cm) of oil into a medium wok and place over medium-high heat. Test the oil to make sure it is hot by dropping a pinch of the batter into the oil. If the batter rises quickly to the top, the oil is hot and ready. If not, let the oil heat longer.
7 When the oil is hot, mix the batter and place a heaping spoonful of the battered spinach and fenugreek in the wok. Fry until the fritter is crisp and the batter turns golden, turning frequently, about 2½ minutes. You may fry these in batches, depending on the size of your wok, but do not overcrowd the wok.
8 Remove the fritters from the oil with a slotted spoon or spider and place on paper towels to drain any excess oil. Place all the fritters on a platter and enjoy!

How to Make the Spinach and Fenugreek Fritters

FIRST Chopped spinach and and fenugreek leaves mixed in the batter and set aside to rest for 10 minutes. **SECOND** Placing a heaping spoonful of the battered spinach and fenugreek into the oil. **THIRD** Fry these up in batches until crisp and golden brown; remove and place on a paper towel to drain the excess oil.

Tomato Soup

My mother's garden generously produces tomatoes, and even after sharing with friends and neighbors, there are plenty left over. My mom makes a wonderful, light tomato broth soup that gives a warm tickle inside as you sip it.

Serves 2 to 3
Prep time: 10 minutes
Cook time: 35 minutes
Refrigerator life: 3 days
Reheating method: Place the refrigerated soup in a microwave, cover and stir periodically. Or, place it in a saucepan over medium-low heat and stir periodically.

6 fully ripe tomatoes, washed and cut in half
3 cups (750 ml) water
1 teaspoon salt
1 teaspoon ground black pepper

1 Place the halved tomatoes in a large saucepan. Add the water and cover the saucepan. Bring to a rolling boil over high heat. Boil for 15 minutes.
2 Reduce the heat to medium. Simmer covered for 10 minutes.
3 Turn off the heat and let it cool for 10 minutes.
4 Pour the boiled tomatoes into a large sieve placed over a large bowl. Using the back of a large spoon, press the tomatoes to squeeze out the juice. Discard the squeezed tomato flesh.
5 Add the salt and black pepper to the juice and mix together. Pour into small glasses or coffe cups and serve.

Spicy Sweet Potatoes

There are many different varieties of sweet potatoes, often called yams in America, although true yams are a different variety of plants species common in South and Central America. In India, sweet potatoes are boiled, cubed, and tossed with lime juice and a few spices and served with toothpicks as a tasty street food. Sweet potatoes are high in vitamin A, which is good for healthy vision and good skin.

Serves 4
Prep time: 5 minutes
Cook time: 25 minutes
Refrigerator life: 1 hour (Tastes best freshly tossed and served.)

2 medium sweet potatoes (total 1 lb/500 g)
½ teaspoon ground red pepper (cayenne)
½ teaspoon salt
½ teaspoon ground black pepper
Juice of 2 limes

1 Wash the unpeeled potatoes with cold water and place them in a large saucepan. Cover them with about 1 inch (2.5 cm) of water, making sure that the level of the water is at least 2 inches (5 cm) from the top of the saucepan so that the water does not boil over. Cover the saucepan. Bring to a rolling boil over high heat.
2 Reduce the heat to medium-high. Continue boiling covered for about 20 minutes, or until you can easily insert a knife into the potato.
3 Drain the potatoes in a colander and let the potatoes cool slightly so you can handle them, or you can run cold water over them to cool them faster.
4 Using your fingers or a small knife, peel the skin off the potatoes and discard. Cut the potatoes into ½-inch (1.25 cm) cubes.
5 Place the cubed potatoes in a medium serving bowl. Add the red pepper, salt, black pepper, and lime juice. Mix well and serve.

Dad's Quick & Easy Microwaved Hot Potatoes (Sweet Potatoes, New Potatoes and Russet Potatoes)

My dad enjoys his quick and easy method to cook potatoes in a microwave. He is very enthusiastic about making and sharing them, and wanted to make sure I give you instructions for his easy way of enjoying potatoes. Even if you have never cooked before, you can now learn to make this quick and tasty snack. Shop for firm, wrinkle free potatoes. You can store potatoes in a cool pantry for about one week.

Quick Sweet Potatoes

In India, whole sweet potatoes are often cooked by being buried in hot ashes. When done, the skin is peeled off and the sweet flesh is enjoyed. The modern day version is to cook them in the microwave as my dad does.

1 Washes 2 medium sweet potatoes (total 1 lb/500 g) and pat dry. Wrap them together in a kitchen towel and puts them in the microwave for 4 minutes, turning halfway between.
2 To see if they are done, press the towel to feel if the sweet potatoes are soft. You can also put a fork in it and see if it easily goes through. If not, continue to microwave them in 1 minute intervals, checking to see if they are done after each additional minute.
3 When they are done, the skins will be wrinkled. Remove from the microwave, unwrap the sweet potatoes, and place on a plate. Cut each potato lengthwise in half and enjoy it with a fork while still warm.

Quick New Potatoes

New potatoes are simply young potatoes of any variety. They have a waxy texture and thin skins, and retain they shape well after cooking.

1 Wash 8 new potatoes (red, white, purple Peruvian) or a combination). Do not peel the potatoes. The skin is thin, so it's edible. Pat them dry. Wrap them together in a kitchen towel and place them in the microwave for 4 minutes.
2 Turn the potatoes and microwave for 6 minutes more. To see if they are done, press the towel to feel if potatoes are soft. You can also put a fork in it and see if it easily goes through. It not, continue to microwave them in 1 minute intervals, checking to see if they are done after each additional minute.
3 When they are done, the skins will be wrinkled. Remove from the microwave and cut each potato into 4 pieces. Spread the pieces on a plate.
4 Cut up 1 tablespoon of unsalted butter (or vegan buttery spread) and sprinkle on top of the potatoes. Evenly sprinkle on the juice of ½ lime and ¼ teaspoon each of salt and black pepper. Enjoy!

Quick Baked Russet Potatoes

Russet potatoes, also called Idaho potatoes, baking potatoes, and old potatoes, have brown skin and white flesh. They are a very versatile potato that I use in most of my cooking.

1 Wash 2 medium russet potatoes (total 1 lb/500 g). Pat them dry. Wrap them together in a kitchen towel and place them in the microwave for 7 minutes, turning halfway between.
2 To see if they are done, press the towel to feel if potatoes are soft. You can also put a fork in it and see if it easily goes through. If not, continue to microwave them in 1 minute intervals, checking to see if they are done after each minute.
3 When they are done, the skins will be wrinkled. Remove from the microwave and cut each potato lengthwise in half. Cut each half lengthwise in half again.
4 Cut up 1 tablespoon of unsalted butter (or vegan buttery spread) and sprinkle on top of the potatoes. Evenly sprinkle on the juice of 1 lime and ¼ teaspoon each of salt and black pepper. Use a fork to mash the potato so the butter will melt in and the seasonings will mix together. Enjoy!

Potato Cutlets

Potato cutlets are breaded patties often served in restaurants in India. They make excellent appetizers at a dinner party. You may serve these cutlets with Fresh Coriander Chutney (page 37) or even with ketchup. My mom used to pack me a vegetarian burger for my school lunch with a potato cutlet, lettuce, tomato, cheese, ketchup, and mustard between a hamburger bun. Potatoes are rich in carbohydrates, thus giving us an energy boost.

Makes 8 cutlets
Prep time: 5 minutes + 35 minutes to boil the potatoes (can be done 1 day in advance)
Cook time: 9 minutes
Refrigerator Life: 3 days, but tastes best freshly made and served hot
Reheating Method: Place the refrigerated cutlets in a warmed oven (about 350°F) and heat. A less preferred method is to heat the cutlets in a microwave.

2 medium russet potatoes (total 1 lb/500 g), boiled and peeled (see page 22)
¼ teaspoon ground red pepper (cayenne)
1 teaspoon salt
¾ teaspoon ground black pepper
½ teaspoon cumin seeds
1 fresh finger-length green chili pepper, finely diced (any variety)
1 handful fresh coriander leaves (cilantro) (about ¼ cup/10 g packed leaves), rinsed and chopped
¼ cup (30 g) plain bread crumbs
5 tablespoons vegetable oil

1 In a medium bowl, mash the peeled potatoes with one hand or a potato masher until there are no lumps. Add the red pepper, salt, black pepper, and cumin seeds. Mix to combine.

2 Add the green chili pepper and coriander leaves. Using one hand, mix to combine. Taste a small bit of the potato mixture to make sure the seasonings and spices are to your liking and add more if desired.

3 Divide the mixture into 8 equal parts. Using your palms, form 8 oval patties about ½ inch (1.25 cm) thick each. Make sure to compress the patties tightly in your palms so they will not fall apart while cooking.

4 Place the bread crumbs on a small plate. Generously dip all sides of each patty in the breadcrumbs. Discard left over crumbs.

5 Spread 2 tablespoons of the oil into a large nonstick skillet and place over medium heat. When the oil is heated, add the cutlets. Cook for 2 minutes.

6 Add 1 more tablespoon of the oil to the skillet, around the bottom of the cutlets Cook for 2 more minutes and then, using a spatula, gently flip the cutlets. The flipped side will be golden to dark brown and a bit crisp.

7 Add 2 tablespoons more of the oil to the skillet around the bottom of the cutlets. Cook for 4 minutes.

8 Flip the cutlets once more and cook for an additional 1 minute. Enjoy!

Opo Squash Fritters

When the tender flesh of opo squash is grated and mixed with gluten-free gram flour (chickpea flour or *besan*), it can be rolled into small balls and fried to create a savory, elegant fritters. Opo squash, also known as bottle gourd, is a mild summer squash popular throughout India, where it is called *kaddu, dudhi, lauki,* or *ghiya*. Choose small opo squash when they are still young and tender and do not have many seeds yet, or just very soft edible seeds. They may be refrigerated in a plastic bag for up to three days.

Makes 12 opo squash fritters
Prep time: 15 minutes
Cook time: 3 minutes
Refrigerator Life: Not recommended. (Tastes best freshly friend and served hot.)

1 small opo squash (about 1½ lbs/700 g)
1 teaspoon salt
¼ cup (25 g) + 3 tablespoons gram flour
¼ teaspoon ground red pepper (cayenne)
¼ teaspoon ground black pepper
½ teaspoon peeled and finely grated fresh ginger
Canola oil, for deep-frying

1 Wash and peel the opo squash with a vegetable peeler. Cut off both ends and discard. Taste a bit of the squash to make sure it is not bitter. If it is bitter, use another opo squash. Using a box grater, grate the opo squash on the small grating holes until you get about 2 cups (300 g) of grated squash. Wrap any extra squash in plastic wrap and put in the refrigerator for up to 2 days. If there are seeds, they should be soft and tender and you can include them. If the center of the opo squash is too soft to grate, you can use the large grating holes.

2 Place grated squash and ¾ teaspoon of the salt in a medium bowl. Using one hand, mix to combine. Place the grated squash into a large sieve placed over a bowl. Using the back of a spoon, press the squash to squeeze out the water. If making Opo Squash Dumpling Curry (page 95), save the squeezed water, which should be about ½ cup (65 ml). If not, you may discard the water now.

3 Pour ½ inch (1.25 cm) of oil into a medium wok and place over medium-high heat. While the oil is heating up, place the flour, red pepper, black pepper, and the remaining ¼ teaspoon of the salt in a medium bowl. Mix together. Add the shredded squash and ginger. Using one hand, mix everything together.

4 Separate the mixture into 12 equal pieces. Roll each piece between your hands to form a smooth ball. The mixture will be very soft.

5 Before frying the fritters, test the oil to make sure it is hot by pinching a piece of the mixture from a ball and dropping into the oil. If the mixture rises quickly to the top with bubbles around it, the oil is hot and ready. It not, let the oil heat longer.

6 When the oil is hot, gently drop each ball into the wok. Deep fry the ball until they have turned golden brown, turning frequently, about 3 minutes.

7 Remove the balls from the oil with a slotted spoon and place them in a wide bowl lined with paper towels to drain any excess oil.

8 Place the balls on a platter and enjoy now while they are warm and slightly crisp on the outside and soft and tender on the inside. Serve with Fresh Coriander Chutney (page 37) for dipping.

How to Make the Opo Squash Fritters

FIRST Grated opo squash mixed with gram flour, spices, and ginger. **SECOND** Grated opo squash rolled into balls and ready to fry. **THIRD** Deep fry the Opo Squash Fritters in a wok.

CHAPTER 3

Breads and Rice

Grains are nature's gift and can be enjoyed whole, processed into different stages, or ground to give us flour. Depending on how grains are processed, their nutritional value, cook time, and taste varies. Whole grains, such as brown rice and quinoa, are the most nutritious, meaning the entire grains are used. When whole grains are ground up, they create nutritious flours, such as whole wheat flour, that we can use to make delicious breads.

Breads and rice have beneficial vitamins and minerals and are a major source of carbohydrates, and fiber. Breads and rice are the staples of Indian meals. Breads can be eaten along with your meal, and some breads are the meal themselves, tasting wonderful with a side of plain yogurt.

Indian breads are eaten by tearing away pieces with your fingers, and using it to grab the main dish or scoop up a curry. Many Indian breads are made with chapati flour, a whole-wheat flour made from finely ground and sifted whole durum wheat, although you can easily substitute a mix of common whole wheat flour and all-purpose flour. Although naan might be the bread that first comes to mind when thinking about Indian breads, the most common everyday bread made in Indian homes is Baked Whole Wheat Flatbreads (page 54), which is cooked using a cast-iron skillet. *Paratha* are flatbreads that are cooked with a bit of oil and are made on a skillet as well.

Rice is such a wonderful grain that can round off a meal, or be a meal by itself. Basic white rice can be served with any dish, although I prefer to eat rice with curried dishes, or dishes that have a saucy base to them so they mix well. Rice and quinoa may be quickly cooked to into one-pot meals, such as Vegetable Rice Pilaf (page 65) and Quinoa Cashew Pilaf (page 60). When putting together your meal, you may serve either a bread or a rice, or even both along with the other dishes.

Baked Whole Wheat Flatbreads

Chapati, also known as *roti*, is a whole wheat flatbread, which is similar to the Mexican whole wheat tortilla. Like most Indians from the northern region of India, I grew up eating hot *chapatis* with dinner as the basic bread of the meal.

Makes 8 flatbreads

Prep time: 15 minutes + 30 minutes resting (dough can be made up to 2 days in advance)

Cook time: 80 seconds per flatbread

Refrigerator life: 2 days, but tastes best freshly made and served hot

Freezer life: 1 month (Place a sheet of parchment paper between each flatbread before freezing to prevent them from sticking to each other. Then place the stack in an airtight container, plastic bag or tightly wrapped in foil)

Reheating Method: Place the refrigerated or defrosted flatbread in the microwave and heat. Or, place the bread on a skillet on medium-high heat, flipping frequently

1¼ cups (150 g) chapati flour (substitute 1 cup/120 g whole wheat flour plus ¼ cup/30 g all-purpose flour), plus extra flour for dusting

½ cup (125 ml) water

2 teaspoons vegetable oil (optional)

Making and Forming the Dough

1 Place the flour and water in a medium bowl. Using one hand, thoroughly knead the dough for about 5 minutes, using all the loose flour to form a soft and smooth dough. Shape the dough into a ball.

2 Moisten the inside of a clean bowl with water and place the dough ball in the bowl. Cover and let rest at room temperature for 30 minutes, or you may refrigerate up to 2 days.

3 Knead the rested dough for 1 minute. If the dough was refrigerated, let the dough come to room temperature to make it easier to knead. (If the dough is too sticky, dust with a bit of loose flour as needed.)

4 Place a large cast-iron skillet (with a low rim to allow easy flipping) over high heat.

5 While the skillet is heating up, separate the dough into 8 equal pieces. Roll each piece between your hands to form a smooth ball and then slightly flatten it between your palms.

6 Working with 1 flattened dough ball at a time, dip both sides of the flattened dough ball in loose flour. Place on a flat rolling surface. Using a rolling pin, roll out the dough ball into a circle about 5 inches (12.5 cm) across. You may flip and turn the circle while gently rolling to help you get an even thickness and a round shape. Dust with loose flour as needed, but try to use as little extra flour as possible.

Cooking the Flatbread

1 When the skillet is hot, carefully slide the rolled-out circle onto your palm and place it on the skillet. The skillet must be hot; otherwise the bread will become dry and hard. Cook for about 30 seconds, and then using a spatula, flip the bread. There should be some brown spots on the flipped side.

2 Cook for about 20 seconds and flip again. There should be brown spots on the flipped side.

3 Cook for 15 seconds, pressing down on the bread with the spatula to encourage the bread to puff up, and flip again.

4 Cook 15 seconds, pressing down on the bread with the spatula to ensure the bread is well cooked. Remove the puffed bread from the skillet. If desired, lightly spread ¼ teaspoon of the oil on it.

5 Continue to roll out and cook the remaining dough balls. Enjoy now or stack them and wrap tightly in foil to keep them warm until ready to serve. You may also refrigerate or freeze for later!

TIP When rolling out dough to make Indian breads, it is best to use as little loose flour for dusting as possible because the flour will burn and become grainy as the dough cooks. Traditionally, the dough is slapped between the palms before putting it on the skillet to shake off any excess loose flour, but this comes with a lot of practice and creates a bit of a mess! An easier way to decrease the amount of flour on the breads is to wipe any loose flour off your work surface before rolling out the next bread. Also, wipe the skillet with a dry cloth or paper towel after each bread is removed to prevent any loose flour on the skillet from sticking to the next bread as it cooks. Making flatbreads can get a bit messy and it may be hard to roll out a perfect circle, but don't worry about the shape, but do try to get an even thickness for proper cooking. I simplify my life by often just buying Mexican whole wheat tortillas and heating them directly on the gas stove burner or on a cast-iron skillet over medium-high heat to get similar results!

How to Cook the Flatbreads

FIRST The rolled-out dough circle is carefully placed on a hot skillet. **SECOND** There will be brown spots on the bread after flipping it. **THIRD** Pressing down on the bread with the spatula will encourage the bread to puff up.

Daikon Stuffed Wheat Flatbreads

Daikon, also called white radish, is the Japanese name for this root vegetable that looks like a huge white carrot. In Hindi, daikon is called *mooli*. Daikon has a sharp peppery flavor and a pungent aroma. My mom grates daikon and stuffs it between whole wheat dough to create daikon stuffed flatbreads, called *mooli ka paratha*.

Makes 4 daikon stuffed flatbreads

Prep time: 15 minutes + 30 minutes resting (dough can be made up to 2 days in advance)

Cook time: 3 minutes per flatbread

Refrigerator Life: 2 days, but tastes best freshly made and served hot

Freezer Life: 1 month (Place a sheet of parchment paper between each flatbread before freezing to prevent them from sticking to each other. Then place the stack in an airtight container, plastic bag or tightly wrapped in foil)

Reheating Method: Place the refrigerated or frozen flatbread in the microwave and heat. Or, place the flatbread on a skillet over medium-high heat, flipping frequently.

2 tablespoons vegetable oil
4 thin pats of butter or vegan buttery spread

DOUGH

1¼ cups (150 g) chapati flour (substitute 1 cup/120 g) whole wheat flour plus ¼ cup/30 g all-purpose flour), plus extra flour for dusting
½ cup (125 ml) water

FILLING

2 medium daikons (total 1 lb/500 g)
½ teaspoon ground red pepper (cayenne)
1 teaspoon salt
½ teaspoon ground black pepper
Juice of ½ lime

Making the Dough

1 Place the flour and water in a medium bowl. Using one hand, thoroughly knead the mixture for about 5 minutes, using up all of the loose flour to form a soft and smooth dough. Shape the dough into a ball.

2 Wet the inside of a clean bowl with water and place the dough ball in the bowl. Cover and let rest at room temperature for 30 minutes, or you may refrigerate up to 2 days. Just before you're ready to cook the bread, prepare the filling.

Making the Filling

1 Wash and peel the daikons with a vegetable peeler. Cut off both ends and discard. Using a box grater, shred each daikon on the small grating holes.

2 Squeeze out the water of the grated daikon by grabbing a handful at a time and squeezing it over the sink.

3 Place the squeezed daikon in a medium bowl. Add the red pepper, salt, black pepper, and lime juice. Using one hand, mix to combine.

4 Divide the filling into 4 equal parts.

Assembling and Cooking the Flatbreads

1 Knead the rested dough for 1 minute. If the dough was refrigerated, let the dough come to room temperature for easier kneading. (If the dough is too sticky, dust with a bit of loose flour.)

2 Place a large cast iron skillet (with a low rim to allow easy flipping) over high heat.

3 While the skillet is heating up, separate the dough into 8 equal pieces. Roll each piece between your hands to form a smooth ball and then slightly flatten it between your palms.

4 Work with 2 flattened dough balls at a time to make one flatbread. Dip both sides of each flattened dough ball in loose flour. Place them on a flat rolling surface. Using a rolling pin, gently roll out both dough balls into circles about 4 inches (10 cm) across. You may flip and turn the circles while rolling to help you get an even thickness and a round shape. Dust with loose flour as needed, but try to use as little extra flour as possible.

5 Evenly spread ¼ teaspoon of the oil on each rolled out circle.

6 Place 1 part of the daikon filling in the center of 1 rolled out circle. Using your fingers, evenly spread out the filling on the dough circle, almost to the edges.

7 Place the other dough circle on top of the one with the filling, oiled side down. Pinch together the edges of the 2 circles to seal them and keep the filling from coming out. Dust both sides of the sealed dough with loose flour.

8 Using a rolling pin, very gently roll out the dough to form a 6.5-inch (16.25 cm) circle. You may flip and turn the circle while rolling to help you get an even thickness and a round shape. Dust with extra flour as needed.

9 When the skillet is hot, carefully slide the rolled out circle onto your palm and place it on the skillet. The skillet must be hot; otherwise the bread will become dry and hard. Cook for about 1 minute, and then using a spatula, flip the bread. There should be some brown spots on the flipped side.

10 Cook for about 1 minute and flip again. There should be brown spots on the flipped side. Spread 1 teaspoon of the oil evenly on the bread.

11 Flip it and cook for 30 seconds.

12 Flip once more and cook for an additional 30 seconds.

13 Remove the bread from the skillet.

14 Continue to roll out and cook the remaining dough. Enjoy now or stack them and wrap tightly in foil to keep them warm until ready to serve. Serve with a pat of butter on top of each hot bread. You may also refrigerate or freeze for later.

Opo Squash Flatbreads

Opo squash, also known as bottle gourd, is a mild summer squash popular throughout India, where it is called *kaddu*, *dudhi*, *lauki*, or *ghiya*, depending on the region. It is ideal to use them when they are young and tender and do not have many seeds yet, or just very tender edible seeds. Opo squash can be shredded and kneaded into chickpea flour dough to make a wonderful flatbread called *ghiya paratha*.

Makes 8 opo squash flatbreads

Prep time: 15 minutes

Cook time: about 1 minute per flatbread

Refrigerator life: 2 days, but tastes best freshly made and served hot

Freezer life: 1 month (Place a sheet of parchment paper between each flatbread before freezing to prevent them from sticking to each other. Then place the stack in an airtight container, plastic bag, or tightly wrap in foil.)

Reheating method: Place the refrigerated or reheated flatbread in a microwave and heat. Or, place the flatbread on a skillet over medium-high heat, flipping frequently.

1 small opo squash (about 1½ lbs/700 g)
2 teaspoons salt
1¼ cups (150 g) chapati flour (substitute 1 cup/120 g whole wheat flour plus ¼ cup/30 g all-purpose flour), plus extra flour for dusting
¾ teaspoon ground red pepper (cayenne)
½ teaspoon ground black pepper
2 teaspoons peeled and finely grated fresh ginger
4 tablespoons plus 2 teaspoons vegetable oil
3 tablespoons squash water (Step 2)

Making the Dough

1 Wash and peel the opo squash with a vegetable peeler. Cut off both ends and discard. Taste the squash and if it's bitter use another opo squash. Using a box grater, grate the opo squash on the large grating holes until you get about 2 cups (300 g). Wrap any extra squash in plastic wrap and refrigerate for up to 2 days. If the seeds are soft and tender they can be included.

2 Place grated squash and salt in a medium bowl. Using one hand, mix to combine. Place the grated quash into a large sieve placed over a bowl. Using the back of a spoon, press the squash to squeeze out the water. You should get about ½ cup (125 ml) of the squash water. Save the water for the next step.

3 Place the flour, red pepper, and black pepper in a medium bowl. Mix together. Add the shredded squash, ginger, 2 tablespoons of the oil ,and 3 tablespoons of the squeezed squash water. Using one hand, thoroughly knead the mixture for about 5 minutes, using up all of the loose flour to form a smooth and slightly firm dough.

Discard the remaining squash water.

4 Place a large cast-iron skillet (with a low rim to allow easy flipping) over high heat.

Forming the Dough

1 While the skillet is heating up, separate the dough into 8 equal pieces.

2 Roll each piece between your hands to form a smooth ball and then slightly flatten it between your palms.

3 Working with one flattened dough ball at a time, dip both sides of the dough in loose flour. Place on a flat rolling surface. Using a rolling pin, gently roll out the dough ball into a circle about 4 inches (10 cm) across. You may flip and turn the circle while rolling it to get an even thickness and a round shape. Dust with loose flour as needed, but try to use as little extra flour as possible.

4 Spread ½ teaspoon of oil evenly on the rolled-out circle.

5 Fold the top part of the circle halfway down.

6 Fold the bottom part of the circle over the top fold.

7 Fold the left part to the center.

8 Fold the right side over the left fold to form a square.

9 Slightly flatten the square by gently pressing down on it with your fingers. Dip both side of the square in loose flour. Place on a flat rolling surface. Use a rolling pin, gently roll out the dough square into about a 5-inch (12.5-cm) square.

10 You may flip and turn the square while rolling to get an even thickness. Dust with loose flour as needed, but try to keep it at a minimum.

Cooking the Flatbreads

1 When the skillet is hot, carefully slide the rolled-out square onto your palm and place it on the skillet. The skillet must be hot; otherwise the bread will become dry and hard. Cook for about 30 seconds, and then using a spatula, flip the bread. There should be some small brown spots on the bread.

2 Cook for about 30 seconds and flip again. There should be small brown spots on the flipped side.

3 Spread ½ teaspoon of the oil evenly on the bread and flip it.

4 Cook for 5 seconds, pressing down on the brad with a spatula, and flip again.

5 Cook for 5 seconds, pressing down on the bread with a spatula. Remove the bread from the skillet.

6 Continue to roll out and cook the remaining dough. Enjoy now or stack them and wrap tightly in foil to keep them warm until ready to serve. You may also refrigerate or freeze for later!

How to make the Opo Squash Flatbreads

FIRST Spread the oil evenly on the rolled-out dough circle. **SECOND** Fold the top part of the circle halfway down. **THIRD** Fold the bottom part of the circle over the top fold.

FOURTH Fold the left part to the center. **FIFTH** Fold the right side over the left fold to form a square. **SIXTH** Rolled out square ready to cook.

1 cup (180 g) uncooked white quinoa
3 tablespoons vegetable oil
20 whole cashews, split in half lengthwise
1 teaspoon cumin seeds
1 small onion, thinly sliced into half-moons
1 medium russet potato (about ½ lb/ 225 g), peeled and diced into ¼ in (6 mm) cubes
2 medium carrots, peeled and diced into ¼ in (6 mm) cubes
½ cup (60 g) frozen or fresh green peas
2 cups (500 ml) water
1 teaspoon salt
¼ teaspoon ground turmeric

1 Place the quinoa in a large sieve. Run cold water over it to thoroughly wash the grains. While washing the quinoa, rub the grains with your fingers to thoroughly clean them. Drain the quinoa.

2 Pour 1 tablespoon of the oil in a medium saucepan and place it over medium heat. When the oil is heated, add the cashews. Sauté until the cashews are light golden, stirring frequently, about 30 seconds. Remove the cashews from the saucepan and place aside.

3 Pour the remaining 2 tablespoons of the oil into the medium saucepan and place it over medium heat. When the oil is heated, add the cumin seeds and onion. Sauté the onion until lightly golden, stirring frequently, about 5 minutes.

4 Add the sautéed cashews, potato, carrot, peas, and quinoa. Stir to combine. Cook for 3 minutes, stirring frequently.

5 Add the water, salt, and turmeric. Stir to combine. Bring to a rolling boil over high heat.

6 Stir and reduce the heat to medium-low. Cover the saucepan. Simmer undisturbed until the water is completely absorbed and you do not see any more water on the bottom of the saucepan, about 13 minutes. The grains will have turned slightly transparent, and the spiral-like germ will have separated from the grain and curl around it like a small thread.

7 Turn off the heat. Let rest, covered, for 5 minutes on the warm stove. Keep covered until ready to serve or let cool to room temperature and refrigerate or freeze for later. Before serving, gently fluff the quinoa with a fork to mix the cashews and vegetables.

Quinoa Cashew Pilaf

If you have not yet tried or know what quinoa (pronounced keen-wah) is, you may have still heard about this nutritious gluten-free grain. Quinoa is a plant-based complete protein, meaning it has all of the essential amino acids to make the proteins our body needs. This tiny bead shaped grain is all the rage, especially among mothers of vegetarian children. My friends Monica and Angela often pack a quinoa dish for their children on our playdate outings. I hope they will enjoy my pilaf-style recipe in which I cook the quinoa with tempered cumin seeds, vegetables, and cashews. I love when my daughter asks me to pack quinoa for her school lunch...it is so cute to hear her clearly say "quinoa!" This dish can be eaten as a side dish, or even a light meal.

Serves 4
Prep time: 10 minutes
Cook time: 25 minutes + 5 minutes to rest
Refrigerator life: 3 days
Freezer life: 1 month
Reheating method: Place the refrigerated or defrosted quinoa in a microwave and stir periodically. Or, place the quinoa in a saucepan, and warm over medium-low heat, stirring periodically.

Indian Cornbread

Indian cornbread served along with Mixed Greens (page 98) sprinkled with some jaggery (unrefined cane sugar) is a popular meal from the northern Indian state of Punjab. Growing up, it was always a treat when my mom made this for a meal in the cooler months.

Makes 6 cornbread discs
Prep time: 15 minutes
Cook time: about 1½ minutes per flatbread
Refrigerator life: 2 days, but tastes best freshly made and served hot
Freezer life: 1 month (Place a sheet of parchment paper between each flatbread before freezing to prevent them from sticking to each other. Then place the stack in an airtight container, plastic bag, or tightly wrap in foil.)
Reheating method: Place the refrigerated or reheated bread in a microwave and heat. Or, place the bread on a skillet over medium-high heat, flipping frequently.

1 cup (140 g) finely ground yellow cornmeal (also called corn flour)
½ cup (60 g) chapati flour or whole wheat flour, plus extra flour for dusting
1¼ teaspoons carom seeds (*ajwain*) or dried thyme leaves
¾ teaspoon salt
½ cup (125 ml) water
7 tablespoons oil
6 thin pats of unsalted butter (optional)

Making the Dough

1 Place the cornmeal, chapati flour, carom seeds, and salt in a medium bowl. Mix together. Add the water and 6 tablespoons of the oil. Using one hand, thoroughly knead the mixture together for about 2 minutes to form a smooth and soft dough.
2 Place a large cast-iron skillet (with a low rim to allow easy flipping) over high heat.

Forming the Dough

1 While the skillet is heating up, separate the dough into 6 equal pieces.
2 Roll each piece between your hands to form a smooth ball and then slightly flatten it between your palms.
3 Working with one flattened dough ball at a time, dip both sides of the dough in loose flour. Place on a flat surface. Use your fingers and palms to gently pat the dough to flatten it to form a 5-inch (12 cm) circle. You may flip and turn the circle while patting it out to get an even thickness and round shape. If the dough is too soft and breaks, knead in some loose flour.

Cooking the Flatbreads

1 When the skillet is hot, carefully slide the flattened circle onto your palm and place it on the skillet. The skillet must be hot; otherwise the bread will become dry and hard. Cook for about 35 seconds, and then using a spatula, flip the bread. There should be some very small brown spots on the bread.
2 Cook for about 35 seconds and flip again. There should be very small brown spots on the flipped side.
3 Spread ½ teaspoon of the oil evenly on the bread and flip it.
4 Cook for 10 seconds, pressing down on the bread with a spatula, and flip again.
5 Cook for 10 seconds, pressing down on the bread with a spatula. Remove the bread from the skillet.
6 Continue to pat out and cook the remaining dough. Enjoy now or stack them and wrap tightly in foil to keep them warm until ready to serve. Serve with a pat of butter on top of each hot bread. You may also refrigerate or freeze for later.

Fenugreek Cornbreads

Chopped fresh fenugreek leaves kneaded into corn flour can be cooked on your stovetop to make a tasty Indian flatbread called *methi roti*. Fenugreek can be a bit bitter, but when cooked into this cornbread dish and served with butter on top, it's delicious.

Makes 8 fenugreek cornbreads
Prep time: 15 minutes
Cook time: about 1½ minutes per flatbread
Refrigerator life: 2 days, but tastes best freshly made and served hot
Freezer life: 1 month (Place a sheet of parchment paper between each flatbread before freezing to prevent them from sticking to each other. Then place the stack in an airtight container, plastic bag or tightly wrap in foil.)
Reheating method: Place the refrigerated or reheated flatbread in a microwave and heat. Or, place the flatbread on a skillet over medium-high heat, flipping frequently.

½ lb (225 g) fresh fenugreek (about 1 bunch)
1 cup (140 g) finely ground yellow cornmeal (also called corn flour)
½ cup (60 g) chapati flour or whole wheat flour, plus extra flour for dusting
1½ teaspoons carom seeds (*ajwain*) or dried thyme leaves
½ teaspoon ground red pepper (cayenne)
¾ teaspoon salt
4 tablespoons plus 4 teaspoons vegetable oil
¼ cup (65 ml) plus 2 tablespoons water
8 thin pats of unsalted butter or vegan buttery spread

Making the Dough

1 Cut off the stems at the bottom of the fenugreek bunch, where the leafy part ends, and discard. The stems at the bottom of the bunch are not tender like the upper stems. Finely chop the leaves and remaining stems. You should get about 2 cups (130 g) packed leaves. Squeeze the chopped fenugreek with your hands to remove any excess water.
2 Place the cornmeal, chapati flour, carom seeds, red pepper, and salt in a medium bowl. Mix together. Add 4 tablespoons of the oil. Using one hand, mix together. Add the fenugreek leaves and water. Using one hand, thoroughly knead the mixture together for about 5 minutes to form a very soft dough.
3 Place a large cast-iron skillet (with a low rim to allow easy flipping) over high heat.

Forming the Dough

1 While the skillet is heating up, separate the dough into 8 equal pieces.
2 Roll each piece between your hands to form a smooth ball and then slightly flatten it between your palms.
3 Working with one flattened dough ball at a time, generously dip both sides of the dough in loose flour. Place on a flat rolling surface. Use your fingers and palms to gently pat the dough to flatten it to form a 4-inch (10 cm) circle. You may flip and turn the circle while patting it out to get an even thickness and round shape. Using a rolling pin, gently roll out the dough ball into a circle about 4 inches (10 cm) across. Dust with loose flour as needed.

Cooking the Flatbreads

1 When the skillet is hot, carefully slide the flattened circle onto your palm and place it on the skillet. The skillet must be hot; otherwise the bread will become dry and hard. Cook for about 35 seconds, and then using a spatula, flip the bread. There should be some very small brown spots on the bread.
2 Cook for about 35 seconds and flip again. There should be very small brown spots on the flipped side.
3 Spread ½ teaspoon of the oil evenly on the bread and flip it.

4 Cook for 10 seconds, pressing down on the bread with a spatula, and flip again.

5 Cook for 10 seconds, pressing down on the bread with a spatula. Remove the bread from the skillet.

6 Continue to roll out and cook the remaining dough. Enjoy now or stack them and wrap tightly in foil to keep them warm until ready to serve. Serve with a pat of butter on top of each hot bread. You may also refrigerate or freeze for later!

How to Cook the Fenugreek Cornbreads

FIRST The patted-out dough circle is carefully placed on a hot skillet. **SECOND** Brown spots on the bread will appear after flipping it. **THIRD** Press down on the bread with the spatula as it cooks.

Plain Basmati Rice

This is the daily rice that is common in the southern part of India. Dishes from that region tend to be rather spicy, and the rice balances out the spices. I prefer to use Basmati rice, a fragrant long-grained white rice, to make this dish, but in India daily rice is usually made with a less expensive variety of white rice. Basmati rice is typically reserved for more elegant rice dishes such as Vegetable Pilaf Rice (page 65) and Saffron, Fruit, and Nut Rice (page 66). If you prefer to buy plain, long-grained white rice for this dish, that will work as well, but you will miss the fragrance you will get from Basmati rice!

Serves 3 to 4
Prep time: 5 minutes
Cook time: 15 minutes + 5 minutes to rest
Refrigerator life: 3 days
Freezer life: 1 month
Reheating method: Place the refrigerated or defrosted rice in a microwave, sprinkle a few drops of water on it and stir periodically. Or, place the rice in a saucepan, sprinkle a few drops of water on it and warm over medium-low heat, stirring periodically.

1 cup (180 g) uncooked white Basmati rice (or plain-long-grained white rice)
2 cups (500 ml) water

1 Place the rice in a small bowl. Rinse three or four times by repeatedly filling the bowl with cold water and carefully draining off the water. It is okay if the water is not completely clear, but try to get it as clear as you can. Pour the rice into a large sieve to drain.

2 Place the drained rice and 2 cups (500 ml) of water in a medium saucepan. Bring to a rolling boil over high heat.

3 Stir and reduce the heat to low. Cover the saucepan. Simmer undisturbed until the water is completely absorbed and you do not see any more water on the bottom of the saucepan if you insert a spoon through the rice, about 9 minutes. You might see dimples formed on the surface of the rice, which is a sign that the water is completely absorbed.

4 Turn off the heat. Let rest, covered, for 5 minutes on the warm stove. Keep covered until ready to serve or let cool to room temperature and refrigerate or freeze for later. Before serving, gently fluff the rice with a fork. Enjoy!

Variation
Plain Boiled Brown Rice

Brown rice may be used in place of white rice to make a nutritious whole grain dish.

Use 1 cup (180 g) uncooked long-grained brown rice and 2½ (625 ml) cups water. Follow steps 1 through 4 for Plain Basmati Rice, but in step 3, cook for about 35 to 40 minutes, or until there is no more water in the saucepan.

TROUBLESHOOTING TIPS FOR RICE

❁ To avoid burnt rice that sticks to the bottom of the pan, use a heavy bottomed saucepan.

❁ To avoid mushy rice, make sure the rice is simmering after reducing the heat. If it's just sitting in hot water, it will take a long time to cook, and it will become mushy and sticky. Increase the heat if needed so the rice is simmering. If your rice is still mushy, you may have overcooked it. As soon as you do not see any more water on the bottom of the saucepan if you insert a spoon through the rice, turn off the heat.

❁ If you are new to making rice, I would first try making the 1 cup (180 g) amount in the recipe instead of doubling the recipe. Once you get comfortable with making rice, then you can double the recipe, but I never make more than 2 cups (360 g) of rice at one time.

Rice with Cumin and Peas

The delicate hint of cumin and beautiful color of green peas in this rice dish make it my favorite everyday rice. It is quick to make and very flavorful as well. I use Plain Basmati Rice (page 63), which gives this dish added taste, beauty, texture, and fragrance instead of using plain long-grained white rice. This rice dish can be paired with any of the dishes in this book (my favorite pairings are with curries), but it is also flavorful enough to be eaten on its own.

Serves 3 to 4
Prep time: 5 minutes
Cook time: 15 minutes + 5 minutes to rest
Refrigerator life: 3 days
Freezer life: 1 month
Reheating method: Place the refrigerated or defrosted rice in a microwave, sprinkle a few drops of water on it and stir periodically. Or, place the rice in a saucepan, sprinkle a few drops of water on it and warm over medium-low heat, stirring periodically.

1 cup (180 g) uncooked white Basmati rice
2 tablespoons vegetable oil
1 teaspoon cumin seeds
2 cups (500 ml) water
½ teaspoon salt
½ cup (60 g) frozen or fresh green peas

1 Place the rice in a small bowl. Rinse three or four times by repeatedly filling the bowl with cold water and carefully draining off the water. It is okay if the water is not completely clear, but try to get it as clear as you can. Pour the rice into a large sieve to drain.

2 Pour the oil into a medium saucepan and place over medium heat.

3 When the oil is heated, add the cumin seeds and let brown, about 10 seconds. Do not let the cumin seeds burn and turn black.

4 Immediately add the rice and stir thoroughly until all the rice is coated with the oil.

5 Add the water, salt, and peas. Stir to combine. Bring to a rolling boil over high heat.

6 Stir and reduce the heat to low. Cover the saucepan. Simmer undisturbed until the water is completely absorbed and you do not see any more water on the bottom of the saucepan if you insert a spoon through the rice, about 9 minutes. You might see dimples forming on the surface of the rice, which is a sign that the water is completely absorbed.

7 Turn off the heat. Let rest, covered, for 5 minutes on the warm stove. Keep covered until ready to serve or let cool to room temperature and refrigerate or freeze for later. Before serving, gently fluff the rice with a fork to mix the cumin seeds and peas.

Variation

Brown Rice with Cumin and Peas

Use 1 cup (180 g) uncooked long-grained brown rice and 2½ (625 ml) cups water. Follow steps 1 through 5 for Rice with Cumin and Peas, but in step 3, leave out the peas. In step 4, cook for 35 to 40 minutes, or until the water disappears in the saucepan. Gently mix in the peas the last 5 minutes of cooking.

Serves 3 to 4
Prep time: 10 minutes
Cook time: 25 minutes + 5 minutes to rest
Refrigerator life: 3 days
Freezer life: 1 month
Reheating method: Place the refrigerated or defrosted rice in a microwave, sprinkle a few drops of water on it and stir periodically. Or, place the rice in a saucepan, sprinkle a few drops of water on it and warm over medium-low heat, stirring periodically.

1 cup (180 g) uncooked white Basmati rice
4 tablespoons vegetable oil
1 small onion, thinly sliced into half-moons
3 cloves
6 black peppercorns
1 in (2.5-cm) cinnamon stick
1 teaspoon cumin seeds
1 dried bay leaf
3 whole green cardamom pods
½ cup (75 g) green edamame beans or ½ cup (60 g) green beans, fresh or frozen
1½ cups (150 g) fresh or frozen bite-size cauliflower florets (no need to defrost if frozen) (see page 23)
1½ cups (75 g) fresh or frozen bite-size broccoli florets (no need to defrost the frozen ones) (see page 23)
1 medium russet potato (about ½ lb/225 g), peeled and cut into ½ in (1.25 cm) cubes
2 medium carrots, peeled and cut into matchsticks (see page 23)
2 cups (500 ml) water
1¾ teaspoons salt

1 Place the rice in a small bowl. Rinse three or four times by repeatedly filling the bowl with cold water and carefully draining off the water. Try to get the water as clear as you can. Pour the rice into a large sieve to drain.

2 Pour the oil into a large saucepan and place it over medium heat. When the oil is heated, add the onion, cloves, peppercorns, cinnamon stick, cumin seeds, and bay leaf. Open the cardamom pods (see page 20) and add the seeds and the pods. Sauté until the onion is browned

Vegetable Rice Pilaf

A pilaf is a rice dish in which the rice is first lightly browned by cooking it with onions in oil or butter, and then adding in fragrant spices and vegetables. Traditionally in India, this dish uses clarified butter (*ghee*), but I use vegetable oil instead since it is healthier and easily available. You could describe this dish as the Indian version of vegetarian fried rice. My daughter loves both rice and vegetables, especially broccoli. I am so happy when she specifically asks for vegetables and rice and wants me to pack it for her school lunch. I include edamame (green soy beans) in this dish to add protein to this dish. You may eat this one-pot meal rice dish by itself or you may mix in some plain yogurt.

and the edges just start to crisp, stirring frequently, about 8 minutes.

3 Add the edamame (or green peas), cauliflower, broccoli, potato, and carrot. Cover the saucepan and cook for 2 minutes, stirring occasionally.

4 Add the rice. Stir thoroughly. Add the water and salt. Stir to combine. Bring to a rolling boil over high heat.

5 Stir and reduce the heat to low. Cover the saucepan. Simmer undisturbed until

the water is completely absorbed and you do not see any more water on the bottom of the saucepan if you insert a spoon through the rice, about 10 minutes.

6 Turn off the heat. Let rest, covered, for 5 minutes on the warm stove. Keep covered until ready to serve or let cool to room temperature and refrigerate or freeze. Before serving, gently fluff the rice with a fork to mix the vegetables. Leave in the whole spices in for presentation.

Saffron, Fruit, and Nut Rice

You will feel like royalty when eating this elegant, yet very easy to make rice dish with saffron, dried fruit, and nuts. A small amount of saffron gives an exotic aroma and flavor and a beautiful natural yellow tint to the rice. Cashews, almonds, and golden raisins made from dried white (pale green) grapes add rich flavor and texture to this rice dish. You can use other nuts, like walnuts and pistachios.

Serves 3 to 4
Prep time: 5 minutes
Cook time: 15 minutes + 5 minutes to rest
Refrigerator life: 3 days
Freezer life: 1 month
Reheating method: Place the refrigerated or defrosted rice in a microwave, sprinkle a few drops of water on it and stir periodically. Or, place the rice in a saucepan, sprinkle a few drops of water on it and warm over medium-low heat, stirring periodically.

1 cup (180 g) uncooked white Basmati rice
4 tablespoons vegetable oil
½ cup (80 g) golden raisins
¼ cup (30 g) blanched and slivered almonds (see page 21)
½ cup (60 g) cashews, split in half lengthwise
2 cups (500 ml) water
½ teaspoon saffron threads
½ heaping teaspoon salt

1 Place the rice in a small bowl. Rinse three or four times by repeatedly filling the bowl with cold water and carefully draining off the water. It is okay if the water is not completely clear, but try to get it as clear as you can. Pour the rice into a large sieve to drain.

2 Pour the oil into a medium saucepan and place over medium heat. When the oil is heated, add the raisins, almonds, and cashews. Sauté until the cashews are light golden, stirring frequently, about 2 minutes.

3 Add the rice. Stir thoroughly until all of the rice is coated with the oil.

4 Add the water, saffron, and salt. Stir to combine. Bring to a rolling boil over high heat.

5 Stir and reduce the heat to low. The water will have a faint yellow tinge from the saffron. Cover the saucepan. Simmer undisturbed until the water is completely absorbed and you do not see any more water on the bottom of the saucepan when inserting a spoon through the rice, about 8 minutes. You might see dimples formed on the surface of the rice, which is a sign that the water is completely absorbed. The rice will have a faint yellow color to it.

6 Turn off the heat. Let rest, covered, for 5 minutes on the warm stove. Keep covered until ready to serve or let cool to room temperature and refrigerate or freeze for later. Before serving, gently fluff the rice with a fork to mix the dried fruit and nuts.

Mint Rice

This easy and elegant rice dish gets it subtle exotic flavors from fresh mint leaves and onions. It can be served alongside a vegetable dish of your choice, or with a lentil or legume dish. Peppermint and spearmint are the two most common mint varieties. Peppermint has brighter green leaves and a more pungent flavor as compared to spearmint, but either one can be used in this dish. Look for the brightest green leaves when shopping for mint. I store mint in a plastic bag in the refrigerator up to a week, or until it starts discoloring and wilting. I remember as a child having the tedious job of picking mint leaves from my mom's garden when she needed it, and now I pick the leaves from my own garden to make this dish!

Serves 3 to 4
Prep time: 5 minutes
Cook time: 15 minutes + 5 minutes to rest
Refrigerator life: 3 days
Freezer life: 1 month
Reheating method: Place the refrigerated or defrosted rice in a microwave, sprinkle a few drops of water on it and stir periodically. Or, place the rice in a saucepan, sprinkle a few drops of water on it and warm over medium-low heat, stirring periodically.

1 cup (180 g) uncooked white Basmati rice
3 tablespoons vegetable oil
½ onion, thinly sliced into half-moons
½ cup (10 g) packed fresh mint leaves, rinsed and chopped
2 cups (500 ml) water
½ teaspoon salt

1 Place the rice in a small bowl. Rinse three or four times by repeatedly filling the bowl with cold water and carefully draining off the water. It is okay if the water is not completely clear, but try to get it as clear as you can. Pour the rice into a large sieve to drain.

2 Pour the oil into a medium saucepan and place over medium heat. When the oil is heated, add the onion. Sauté until the onion is browned and the edges just start to crisp, stirring frequently, about 7 minutes.

3 Add the rice and mint leaves. Stir thoroughly until all of the rice is coated with the oil.

4 Add the water and salt. Stir to combine. Bring to a rolling boil over high heat.

5 Stir and reduce the heat to low. Cover the saucepan. Simmer undisturbed until the water is completely absorbed and you do not see any more water on the bottom of the saucepan if you insert a spoon through the rice, about 8 minutes. You might see dimples formed on the surface of the rice, which is a sign that the water is completely absorbed.

6 Turn off the heat. Let rest, covered, for 5 minutes on the warm stove. Keep covered until ready to serve or let cool to room temperature and refrigerate or freeze for later. Before serving, gently fluff the rice with a fork to mix the onions and mint leaves.

CHAPTER 4

Lentils and Legumes

Lentils and legumes have been a nutritious food source for thousands of years. Legumes are a class of vegetables with seed pods that include beans, peas, and lentils and are very nutritious. Legumes are low in fat, a good source of energy-rich carbohydrates and rich in protein. They are a healthy substitute for the protein in meat, which has more fat and cholesterol. Lentils and legumes are incomplete proteins, meaning they do not have all the essential amino acids to build protein, but if paired with grains, such as breads or rice in the same meal, the complementary proteins in both dishes combine so our body can make the complete proteins it needs.

Lentils and legumes are also an excellent source of folate, a vitamin that helps the body build new cells. It is an especially important nutrient for women who are either pregnant or planning to become pregnant. The soluble fiber in lentils and legumes helps lower cholesterol and may benefit those at risk for heart disease and diabetes. Lentils and legumes also have potassium, iron, and zinc.

Lentils, called *daal* in Hindi, are a leguminous plant containing flat pods with small edible seeds. The seeds are dried and then may be split and shelled (hulled). Lentils come in a variety of shapes and colors, and when hulled, they reveal different colors and flavors. Lentils can be cooked with water to create a nice thick, soupy dish such as Stewed Split Red Lentils (page 77) and Buttery Black Lentil Stew (page 75). Vegetables, such as zucchini, or leafy greens, such as kale, can be cooked along with lentils to create a heartier dish, such as Split Chickpea and Zucchini Stew (page 73) and Green Lentils and Kale Stew (page 74). You can also sprout whole lentils and toss them with vegetables such as jicama, cucumbers, tomatoes, onions, and some spices and lime juice to create a colorful and nutritious Fresh Lentil Sprout Salad (page 79).

When the seeds of a legume are dried, they are called pulses, such as dried kidney beans, dried black-eyed peas or dried lentils. Legumes such as black beans, chickpeas, kidney beans, and black-eyed peas make nourishing curries that go well with rice dishes or the Baked Whole Wheat Flatbreads (page 54). The soupy consistency of lentil and legumes dishes makes them a perfect accompaniment to sautéed vegetable dishes such as Stuffed Okra (page 92) or Fenugreek and Potatoes (page 93). Lentil and legume dishes may be served along with a meal, or as a soup appetizer, or even a light meal by itself along with some whole grain bread.

Kidney Bean Curry

Rice and beans is a popular and nutritious meal in many cultures around the world. The Indian version of rice and beans is made with kidney beans and traditionally served with rice. Together, this meal is called *rajma chawval*, which means "kidney bean curry and rice" in Hindi. You may also eat this dish with the Baked Whole Wheat Flatbreads (page 54). Kidney beans are firm dark red skinned beans that have an actual kidney shape, with a cream colored flesh. Either canned beans, which is quicker, or dried beans, which have to be soaked overnight and boiled, may be used when cooking this dish.

Serves 4 to 6
Prep time: 10 minutes + overnight soaking (12 hours) if using dried kidney beans
Cook time: 30 minutes + an additional 1 hour 20 minutes if using dried kidney beans
Refrigerator life: 3 days
Freezer life: 1 month
Reheating method: Place the refrigerated or defrosted curry in a microwave, cover and stir periodically. Or, place it in a saucepan over medium-low heat and stir periodically. If the reheated curry seems too thick, you may add a bit of water to it.

NOTE: When buying canned kidney beans it is okay if the container size is approximately 15 ounces (425 g). The amount of liquid in the can varies depending on the brand, so you may add a bit more or less water than the suggested ½ cup (125 ml). I prefer to use the liquid in the can since it has flavor to it and also lends a desirable consistency to the curry in the dish. Try to look for canned beans without the sugar or corn syrup, or squeeze in a little lime juice to balance out the taste. Organic kidney beans are also available.

3 tablespoons vegetable oil
1½ teaspoons minced garlic
1 tablespoon peeled and finely grated fresh ginger
½ small onion, shredded on the largest grating holes of a box grater
1 fully ripe tomato, cut into 4 pieces
¾ teaspoon store bought or homemade Garam Masala (page 109)
¼ teaspoon ground red pepper (cayenne)
¾ teaspoon salt
¾ teaspoon ground black pepper
Two 15 oz (425 g) cans precooked dark red kidneys beans with liquid from cans or 1 cup (180 g) dried dark red kidney beans, soaked overnight and cooked, with 2 cups (500 ml) of the cooking liquid (see page 21)
½ cup (125 ml) water if using canned kidney beans (see note below)

1 Pour the oil into a medium saucepan and place over medium heat. When the oil is heated, add the garlic, ginger, and onion. Sauté until the onion is golden brown, stirring frequently, about 5 minutes.
2 Reduce the heat to medium-low. Add the tomato and cover the saucepan. Cook until the tomato becomes completely soft and mashed and is combined with the onion to form a coarse paste, stirring every minute or so and lightly mashing the tomato, about 5 minutes.
3 Add the Garam Masala, red pepper, salt, and black pepper. Cook uncovered for 6 minutes, stirring frequently.
4 Add the canned kidney beans with their liquid and the additional ½ cup (125 ml) water and bring to a rolling boil over high heat. (Or add the boiled kidney beans with 2 cups (500 ml) of their cooking liquid and bring to a rolling boil over high heat.)
5 Reduce the heat to medium-low. Simmer uncovered for 15 minutes to thicken the curry and let the flavors infuse, stirring occasionally. Enjoy now or let cool to room temperature and refrigerate or freeze for later!

Black Bean Curry

My spicy black bean curry reminds me of an Indian version of a flavorful black bean soup I enjoy when dining out at Mexican and South American restaurants. They are black on the outside with firm cream colored flesh. This dish may be enjoyed with Plain Basmati Rice (page 63), Baked Whole Wheat Flatbreads (page 54), or simply as a soup.

Serves 4 to 6
Prep time: 10 minutes + overnight soaking (12 hours) if using dried beans
Cook time: 30 minutes + an additional 50 minutes if using dried beans
Refrigerator life: 3 days
Freezer life: 1 month
Reheating method: Place the refrigerated or defrosted curry in a microwave, cover and stir periodically. Or, place it in a saucepan over medium-low heat and stir periodically. If the reheated curry seems too thick, you may add a bit of water to it.

3 tablespoons vegetable oil
2 teaspoons minced garlic
1 tablespoon peeled and finely grated fresh ginger
½ small onion, shredded on the largest grating holes of a box grater
1 fully ripe tomato, cut into 4 pieces
1 teaspoon store bought or homemade Garam Masala (page 109)
¼ teaspoon ground red pepper (cayenne)
½ teaspoon salt
1 teaspoon ground black pepper
Two 15 oz (425 g) cans precooked black beans with liquid from cans or 1 cup (180 g) dried dark red kidney beans, soaked overnight and cooked, with 2 cups (500 ml) of the cooking liquid (page 21)
1 cup (250 ml) water if using canned black beans (see note below)

1 Pour the oil into a medium saucepan and place over medium heat. When the oil is heated, add the garlic, ginger, and onion. Sauté until the onion is golden brown, stirring frequently, about 5 minutes.
2 Reduce the heat to medium-low. Add the tomato and cover the saucepan. Cook until the tomato becomes completely soft and mashed and is combined with the onion to form a coarse paste, stirring every minute or so and lightly mashing the tomato, about 5 minutes.
3 Add the Garam Masala, red pepper, salt, and black pepper. Cook uncovered for 6 minutes, stirring frequently.
4 Add the canned kidney beans with their liquid and the additional 1 cup (250 ml) water and bring to a boil over high heat. (Or add the boiled kidney beans with 2 cups (500 ml) of their cooking liquid and bring to a rolling boil over high heat.)

NOTE: When buying canned black beans it is okay if the container size is approximately 15 ounces (425 g). The amount of liquid in the can varies depending on the brand, so you may add a bit more or less water than the suggested 1 cup (250 ml). I prefer to use the liquid in the can since it has flavor to it and also lends a desirable consistency to the curry in the dish. Try to look for canned beans without the sugar or corn syrup, or squeeze in a little lime juice to balance out the taste. Organic black beans are also available.

5 Reduce the heat to medium-low. Simmer uncovered for 15 minutes to thicken the curry and let the flavors infuse, stirring occasionally. Enjoy now or let cool to room temperature and refrigerate or freeze for later!

Black-Eyed Pea Curry

This Black-Eyed Pea Curry, or *rongi*, as my mom calls it in Punjabi, is one of my favorite Indian dishes. This legume gets its name from the tiny black marking in the center of it which actually looks like an eye! You won't believe how easy it is to make a flavorful black-eyed pea curry using precooked and canned black-eyed peas until you try it yourself! For those strict traditionalists, instructions are provided for using dried peas. If you do use dried black-eyed peas, you will have to soak them overnight and then boil them to make them soft. This dish has a saucy consistency and can be eaten with Plain Basmati Rice (page 63) or Rice with Cumin and Peas (page 64) or with Indian breads such as Baked Whole Wheat Flatbreads (page 54).

Serves 4 to 6
Prep time: 10 minutes + overnight soaking (12 hours) if using dried black-eyed peas
Cook time: 30 minutes + an additional hour if using dried black-eyed peas
Refrigerator life: 3 days
Freezer life: 1 month
Reheating method: Place the refrigerated or defrosted curry in a microwave, cover and stir periodically. Or, place it in a saucepan over medium-low heat and stir periodically. If the reheated curry seems too thick, you may add a bit of water to it.

3 tablespoons vegetable oil
1½ teaspoons minced garlic
1 tablespoon peeled and finely grated fresh ginger
1 small onion, shredded on the largest grating holes of a box grater
1 fully ripe tomato, cut into 4 pieces
¼ teaspoon ground turmeric
¼ teaspoon ground red pepper (cayenne)
¾ teaspoon salt
½ teaspoon ground black pepper
Two 15 oz (425 g) cans precooked black-eyed peas with liquid from cans or 1 cup (180 g) dried black-eyed peas, soaked overnight and cooked, with 1½ cups (375 ml) of the cooking liquid (see page 21)
½ cup (125 ml) water if using canned black-eyed peas

1 Pour the oil into a medium saucepan and place over medium heat. When the oil is heated, add the garlic, ginger, and onion. Sauté until the onion is golden brown, stirring frequently, about 5 minutes.

2 Reduce the heat to medium-low. Add the tomato and cover the saucepan. Cook until the tomato becomes completely soft and mashed and then combine it with the onion to form a coarse paste, stirring every minute or so and lightly mashing the tomato, about 5 minutes.

3 Add the turmeric, red pepper, salt, and black pepper. Cook uncovered for 6 minutes, stirring frequently.

4 Add the canned black-eyed peas with their liquid and the additional ½ cup (125 ml) water and bring to a rolling boil over high heat. (Or add the boiled black-eyed peas with 1½ cups (375 ml) of their cooking liquid and bring to a rolling boil over high heat.)

5 Reduce the heat to medium-low. Simmer uncovered for 10 minutes to thicken the curry and let the flavors infuse, stirring occasionally. Enjoy now or let cool to room temperature and refrigerate or freeze for later!

Split Chickpea and Zucchini Stew

This skinned and split chickpea is traditionally made into a stew by simmering it along with peeled and chopped opo squash. I did a switch from the age-old Indian version and used zucchini since it is abundantly available and I like its delicate sweet undertone.

Serves 2 to 3
Prep time: 10 minutes
Cook time: 1 hour
Refrigerator life: 3 days
Freezer life: 1 month
Reheating method: Place the refrigerated or defrosted chickpeas in a microwave, cover and stir periodically. Or, place it in a saucepan over medium-low heat and stir periodically. If it seems too thick, you may add a bit of water to thin it out.

2 small zucchini (total ½ lb/225 g)
½ cup (100 g) dried, skinned and split brown chickpeas (*channa daal*)
5 cups (1.25 liters) water
1 small fully ripe tomato, such as plum (Roma), cut in half
¼ teaspoon ground turmeric
¼ teaspoon ground red pepper (cayenne)
¾ teaspoon salt
2 tablespoons vegetable oil
½ small onion, finely diced
¼ teaspoon cumin seeds

1 Wash the zucchini. Cut off both ends and discard. Do not peel the zucchini. Cut each zucchini into 4 even lengthwise segments. Cut each segment crosswise into ½-inch (1.25 cm) thick pieces.
2 Place the chickpeas on a plate. Sift through them and remove any grit.
3 Transfer the chickpeas to a small bowl. Rinse the chickpeas three times by repeatedly filling the bowl with cold water and carefully draining off the water. It is okay if the water is a bit frothy.
4 Place the chickpeas, 5 cups (1.25 liters) water, tomato, turmeric, red pepper, and salt in a medium saucepan. Stir to combine. Bring to a rolling boil over high heat.
5 Stir and reduce the heat to medium. Cover the saucepan and simmer for 30 minutes, stirring occasionally and lightly mashing the chickpeas with a large wooden spoon as it cooks.

6 Add the zucchini and stir to combine. Cook covered for 20 more minutes or until the chickpeas are completely soft, stirring occasionally. It should not look like the chickpeas are floating individually in the water and you can pick them out; instead it should be similar to a thick soup with an even consistency. Turn off the heat.
7 To temper the spices, pour the oil into a small skillet and place over medium heat. When the oil is heated, add the onion and cumin seeds. Stir to combine. Sauté until the onion is browned, stirring frequently, about 5 minutes.

8 Add the tempered spices to the chickpeas. Stir to combine. Enjoy now or let cool to room temperature or freeze for later. As the stew cools, it will continue to thicken.

Green Lentils and Kale Stew

Fresh kale is cooked along with whole green lentils makes a very nutritious and tasty stew. Kale is a member of the cabbage family and has frilly or curly leaves with a tough stem. In India, green lentils are often cooked with spinach greens, but, instead, I thought this would be an interesting way to use kale.

Serves 2 to 3
Prep time: 10 minutes
Cook time: 1 hour
Refrigerator Life: 3 days
Freezer Life: 1 month
Reheating Method: Put in a microwave, cover and stir periodically. Or, place it in a saucepan over medium-low heat and stir periodically, add water it seems too thick.

½ lb (225 g) fresh kale (about 1 small bunch)
½ cup (100 g) dried whole green lentils (*sabut mung daal*)
5 cups (1.25 liters) water
1 small fully ripe tomato, such as plum (Roma), cut in half
¼ teaspoon ground turmeric
½ teaspoon ground red pepper (cayenne)
¾ teaspoon salt
2 tablespoons vegetable oil
½ small onion, finely diced
¼ teaspoon cumin seeds

1 To de-rib (separating the leaves from the stem) the kale, working with one stem of kale at a time, fold the leaf in half lengthwise. Using a small knife, cut down the length of the stem to separate the leaves from the tough stem. Discard the stems. Coarsely chop the leaves. Put the chopped kale in a colander and wash any of the dirt off with water.

2 Place the lentils on a plate. Sift through them and remove any grit.

3 Transfer the lentils to a small bowl. Rinse the lentils three times by repeatedly filling the bowl with cold water and carefully draining off the water.

4 Place the lentils, 5 cups (1.25 liter) water, tomato, turmeric, red pepper, and salt in a medium saucepan. Hand squeeze the kale to remove any excess water. Add the kale to the saucepan. Stir to combine. Bring to a rolling boil over high heat.

5 Stir and reduce the heat to medium. Cover the saucepan. Simmer until the lentils are completely soft, stirring occasionally and lightly mashing the tomato, about 45 minutes. The lentils should not be floating individually in the water; instead they should come together with the water when fully cooked and should be similar to a thick soup with an even consistency. Add ¼ cup (65 ml) water if it looks like it needs it. Turn off the heat.

6 To temper the spices, pour the oil into a small skillet and place over medium heat. When the oil is heated, add the onion and cumin seeds. Stir to combine. Sauté until the onion is browned, stirring frequently, about 5 minutes.

7 Add the tempered spices to the lentils. Stir to combine. Enjoy now or let cool to room temperature or freeze for later.

Buttery Black Lentil Stew

A popular lentil dish at Indian restaurant buffets is this black lentil stew known as *daal makhani*, meaning buttery lentils. It is made from tiny whole black lentils called black gram, and *sabut urad daal* in Hindi.

Serves 3 to 4

Prep time: 5 minutes + overnight soaking (12 hours)

Cook time: 1 hour 45 minutes

Refrigerator Life: 3 days

Freezer Life: 1 month

Reheating Method: Place the refrigerated or defrosted dish in a microwave, cover and stir periodically. Or, place it in a saucepan over medium-low heat and stir periodically. If it seems too thick, you may add a bit of water to thin it.

½ cup (100 g) dried whole black lentils (*sabut urad daal*)

¼ cup (50 g) dried, skinned and split brown chickpeas (*channa daal*)

10 cups (2.25 liters) water

1 small fully ripe tomato, such as plum (Roma), cut in half

½ teaspoon ground red pepper (cayenne)

1 teaspoon salt

2 tablespoons vegetable oil

½ small onion, finely diced

2 teaspoons peeled and finely grated ginger

1 fresh finger-length green chili pepper, finely chopped (any variety)

2 tablespoons unsalted butter or vegan buttery spread

1 Place the lentils and chickpeas on a plate. Sift through them for grit.

2 Transfer the lentils and chickpeas to a small bowl. Rinse them three times by repeatedly filling the bowl with cold water and carefully draining off the water. Add cold water to cover the lentils. Cover the bowl and let soak overnight at room temperature.

3 The next morning, drain the water from the bowl. Rinse the lentils and chickpeas three times by repeatedly filling the bowl with cold water and carefully draining off the water. If some shells come off, that's okay leave them there.

4 Place the soaked black lentils and chickpeas, 10 cups (2.25 liters) water, tomato, red pepper, and salt in a large saucepan.

Stir to combine. Bring to a rolling boil over high heat, about 15 minutes.

5 Stir and reduce the heat to medium-high. Cover the saucepan and boil for 1 hour, stirring occasionally.

6 With a wooden spoon, lightly mash the lentils against the sides of the saucepan to release their starches and thicken the stew. Cook for 25 more minutes or until the lentils are completely soft, stirring occasionally. The lentils shouldn't be floating individually in the water; instead they should come together with the water when fully cooked and should be similar to a thick soup. Turn off the heat.

7 To temper the spices, pour the oil into a small skillet and place over medium heat. When the oil is heated, add onion, ginger, and green chili pepper. Stir to combine. Sauté until the onion is browned, stirring frequently, about 5 minutes.

8 Add the tempered spices and butter to the lentils. Stir to combine until the butter is melted. Enjoy now or let cool to room temperature or freeze for later.

Stewed Whole Red Lentils

Whole red lentils, called *sabut masoor daal* in Hindi, have a reddish/light brown skin and are orange inside. They are sometimes called brown lentils since their skin has brown shades in it. These lentils can be cooked into an easy lentil stew and be served with the Baked-Whole Wheat Flatbreads (page 54), Plain Basmati Rice (page 63), or Rice with Cumin and Peas (page 64). You may also use Spanish Pardina lentils to make this stew, which look similar to the Indian whole red lentil, but are more grayish/brown in color..

Serves 2 to 3
Prep time: 5 minutes
Cook time: 45 minutes
Refrigerator Life: 3 days
Freezer Life: 1 month
Reheating Method: Place the refrigerated or defrosted dish in a microwave, cover and stir periodically. Or, place it in a saucepan over medium-low heat and stir periodically. If it seems too thick, you may add a bit of water to thin it.

½ cup (100 g) dried whole red lentils (*sabut masoor daal*) or Spanish Pardina lentils
2¾ cups (685 ml) water
1 small fully ripe tomato, such as plum (Roma), cut in half
¼ teaspoon ground turmeric
¼ teaspoon ground red pepper (cayenne)
½ teaspoon salt
2 tablespoons vegetable oil
½ small onion, finely diced
1 fresh finger-length green chili pepper, finely chopped (such as Thai bird's-eye chili pepper, Serrano or jalapeño)
¼ teaspoon cumin seeds

1 Place the lentils on a plate. Sift through them and remove any grit.
2 Transfer the lentils to a small bowl. Rinse the lentils three times by repeatedly filling the bowl with cold water and carefully draining off the water.
3 Place the lentils, 2¾ cups (685 ml) water, tomato, turmeric, red pepper, and salt in a medium saucepan. Stir to combine. Bring to a rolling boil over high heat.
4 Stir and reduce the heat to medium-low. Cover the saucepan. Simmer until the lentils are completely soft, stirring occasionally and lightly mashing the tomato, about 35 minutes. It should not look like the lentils are floating individually in the water and you can pick them out; instead it should be similar to a thick soup with an even consistency. Turn off the heat.
5 To temper the spices, pour the oil into a small skillet and place over medium heat. When the oil is heated, add onion, chili pepper, and cumin seeds. Stir to combine. Sauté until the onion is browned, stirring frequently, about 5 minutes.
6 Add the tempered spices to the lentils. Stir to combine. Enjoy now or let cool to room temperature and freeze for later!

Stewed Split Red Lentils

Split red lentils make one of my favorite lentil dishes since it cooks quickly, and has a nice rich taste to it with the finishing touch of butter! When whole red lentils are skinned and split, they reveal an orange lentil, called *dhuli masoor daal* in Hindi. These orange lentils are also known as "petite crimson lentils" or "red lentils" and surprisingly turn yellowish when cooked (partially due to the turmeric). This stew may be served in individual bowls Baked Whole Wheat Flatbreads (page 54). It can also be spooned over Plain Basmati Rice (page 63) or Rice with Cumin and Peas (page 64).

Serves 2 to 3
Prep time: 5 minutes
Cook time: 25 minutes
Refrigerator Life: 3 days
Freezer Life: 1 month
Reheating Method: Place the refrigerated or defrosted dish in a microwave, cover and stir periodically. Or, place it in a saucepan over medium-low heat and stir periodically. If it seems too thick, you may add a bit of water to thin it.

½ cup (100 g) dried, skinned and split red lentils (*dhuli masoor daal*)
2¼ cups (565 ml) water
1 small fully ripe tomato, such as plum (Roma), cut in half
¼ teaspoon ground turmeric
¼ teaspoon ground red pepper (cayenne)
½ teaspoon salt
1½ tablespoons vegetable oil
½ small onion, finely diced
¼ teaspoon cumin seeds
1 tablespoon unsalted butter or vegan buttery spread
1 handful fresh coriander leaves (cilantro) (about ¼ cup/10 g packed leaves), rinsed and chopped

1 Place the lentils on a plate. Sift through them and remove any grit.
2 Transfer the lentils to a small bowl. Rinse the lentils three times by repeatedly filling the bowl with cold water and carefully draining off the water.
3 Place the lentils, 2¼ cups (565 ml) water, tomato, turmeric, red pepper, and salt in a medium saucepan. Stir to combine. Bring to a rolling boil over high heat.
4 Stir and reduce the heat to medium. Cook for 10 minutes, stirring occasionally and lightly mashing the tomato.
5 Reduce the heat to low and cover the saucepan. Simmer until the lentils are completely soft, stirring occasionally and lightly mashing the tomato, about 5 minutes. It should not look like the lentils are floating individually in the water and you can pick them out; instead they should come together with the water when fully cooked and should be similar to a thick soup with an even consistency. Turn off the heat.
6 To temper the spices, pour the oil into a small skillet and place over medium heat. When the oil is heated, add the onion and cumin seeds. Stir to combine. Sauté until the onion is browned, stirring frequently, about 5 minutes.
7 Add the tempered spices and butter to the lentils. Stir to combine until the butter is melted. Enjoy now or let cool to room temperature or freeze for later! Just before serving, sprinkle the chopped coriander leaves on top.

Chickpea Curry

Cream-colored chickpeas (also called garbanzo beans), or *kabuli channa* in Hindi, make a delicious and nutritious curry dish known as *chana masala*. This bean is also very commonly used in Middle Eastern cuisine and is used to make hummus. You may enjoy this curry with Plain Basmati Rice (page 63), Rice with Cumin and Peas (page 64), or the Baked Whole Wheat Flatbreads (page 54). It is common to offer a small bowl of diced tomatoes, onion and green chili peppers tossed with lime juice, allowing each person to scatter over their curry serving. Either canned beans, which is quicker, or dried beans, which have to be soaked overnight and boiled, may be used when cooking this dish.

Serves 4 to 6

Prep time: 10 minutes + overnight soaking (12 hours) if using dried chickpeas

Cook time: 30 minutes + an additional 50 minutes if using dried chickpeas

Refrigerator life: 3 days

Freezer life: 1 month

Reheating method: Place the refrigerated or defrosted curry in a microwave, cover and stir periodically. Or, place it in a saucepan over medium-low heat and stir periodically. If the reheated curry seems too thick, you may add a bit of water to it.

3 tablespoons vegetable oil

1½ teaspoons minced garlic

1 tablespoon peeled and finely grated fresh ginger

½ small onion, shredded on the largest grating holes of a box grater

1 fully ripe tomato, cut into 4 pieces

¾ teaspoon cumin seeds, roasted and ground (see page 20)

¼ teaspoon ground turmeric

¼ teaspoon ground red pepper (cayenne)

¾ teaspoon salt

½ teaspoon ground black pepper

1 fresh finger-length green chili pepper, finely diced (any variety)

Two 15 oz (425 g) cans precooked chickpeas with liquid from cans or 1 cup (180 g) dried chickpeas, soaked overnight and cooked, with 2 cups (500 ml) of the cooking liquid (see page 21)

¼ cup (65 ml) water if using canned chickpeas (see Note on page 79)

SIDE ACCOMPANIMENTS

½ small onion, diced

1 small fully ripe tomato, such as plum (Roma), diced

1 fresh finger-length green chili pepper, sliced into thin rings (any variety)

Juice of 1 lime

1 Pour the oil into a medium saucepan and place over medium heat. When the oil is heated, add the garlic, ginger, and onion. Sauté until the onion is golden brown, stirring frequently, about 5 minutes.

2 Reduce the heat to medium-low. Add the tomato and cover the saucepan. Cook until the tomato becomes completely soft and mashed and is combined with the onion to form a coarse paste, stirring every minute or so and lightly mashing the tomato, about 5 minutes.

3 Add the cumin, turmeric, red pepper, salt, black pepper, and green chili pepper. Cook uncovered for 6 minutes, stirring frequently.

4 Add the canned chickpeas with their liquid and the additional ¼ cup (65 ml) water and bring to a rolling boil over high heat. (Or add the boiled chickpeas with 2 cups (500 ml) of their cooking liquid and bring to a rolling boil over high heat.)

5 Reduce the heat to medium-low. Simmer uncovered for 15 minutes to thicken the curry and let the flavors infuse, stirring occasionally. Enjoy now or let cool to room temperature and refrigerate or freeze for later! Before serving, prepare the Side Accompaniments to sprinkle over individual helpings. Place the onion, tomato, green chili pepper, and lime juice in a small bowl and toss.

NOTE: When buying canned chickpeas, it is okay if you do not exactly find 15 oz (425 g) cans, as long as they are about that size. The amount of liquid in the can varies slightly depending on the brand, so you may add a bit more or less water than the suggested ¼ cup (65 ml) to achieve the desired consistency. I prefer to use the liquid in the can since it has flavor to it, just as the cooking liquid (broth) does when boiling dried chickpeas. The liquid in the can also lends consistency of the curry. Organic chickpeas are widely available.

Fresh Lentil Sprout Salad

You can make a colorful and nutritious lentil salad by sprouting whole green lentils, called *sabut mung daal* in Hindi. This beautiful dish makes a healthy snack, or it can be served as a side dish. Sprouted lentils have increased nutritional value due to germination and sprouting. Growing your own mung sprouts is relatively easy and gives you fresh sprouts for your meals.

Serves 4 to 6
Prep time: 15 minutes + overnight soaking (12 hours) + 1 day sitting (24 hours)
Refrigerator Life: 1 hour (tastes best freshly tossed and served.)

½ cup (100 g) dried whole green lentils (*sabut mung daal*)
1 small fully ripe tomato, such as plum (Roma), diced
½ small jicama, peeled and diced, or ½ red bell pepper, diced
5 red radishes, or 1 small turnip, diced
½ small red onion, diced
4 tablespoons peeled and diced cucumber (any variety)
1 handful fresh coriander leaves (cilantro) (about ¼ cup/10 g packed leaves), rinsed and chopped
¼ teaspoon ground red pepper (cayenne)
½ teaspoon salt
½ teaspoon ground black pepper
Juice of 2 limes

1 Place the lentils on a plate. Sift through them and remove any grit.

2 Transfer the lentils to a small bowl. Rinse the lentils three times by repeatedly filling the bowl with cold water and carefully draining off the water. Add cold water to cover the lentils. Cover the bowl and let soak overnight at room temperature.

3 By the next morning, the lentils should be tender. Drain the water from the bowl. Cover the bowl and place aside at room temperature until the following morning. The next morning, you will see long sprouts. At this point, if you are not ready to make the salad, you can cover and refrigerate the sprouted lentils up to 1 day.

4 Place the sprouted lentils and the rest of the ingredients in a serving bowl. Mix to combine. Enjoy now or refrigerate up to 1 hour.

CHAPTER 5

Main Dishes

Vegetables may be grouped according to similar characteristics such as roots, leafy greens, squashes, crucifers, shoot and stalks, bulbs, legumes, and fruit vegetables. Root vegetables are used in Curried Carrots and Peas (page 85) and Mashed Turnips (page 83). Leafy greens are used when making Collard Greens and Parsnips (page 99), or Spinach and Potatoes (page 87). Squash are divided into summer squash and winter squash types. Summer squash are used in the Yellow Squash Curry (page 91) and Opo Squash Dumpling Curry (page 95). Winter squash is used in the Sweet and Spicy Butternut Squash (page 84). Cruciferous vegetables such as cabbage, cauliflower, Brussel Sprouts, and broccoli are known for their bold flavor and high nutritional value. My whole family enjoys eating Sautéed Cauliflower and Potatoes (page 88) and Cabbage and Peas (page 97). Shoots and stalks such as asparagus and celery have edible stems with mild flavors. Bulb vegetables such as onions and garlic are used to create the base for many of my recipes and have amazing flavors that develop while cooking. My favorite vegetable, mushrooms, are edible types of fungi that grow in many different varieties. Sautéed Mushrooms and Peas (page 89) is one way to enjoy the common white mushroom. Fruit vegetables like tomatoes, okra, bitter melon, eggplant, avocados, cucumbers, chilies, peppers, and pea pods are types of fruit but are used as vegetables in the kitchen.

Cut Bell Peppers and Potatoes

Bell peppers are a bell-shaped variety of sweet peppers that come in a range of colors from red, orange, yellow, and green. Sweet peppers are mild and sweet instead of fiery hot. If left on the plant long enough, green bell peppers will fully ripen to a red color and be sweeter. The spice, paprika, is the dried and ground sweet red pepper. Bell peppers cooked with potatoes make an excellent Indian dish (*aloo Shima mirch*) and goes well with Baked Whole Wheat Flatbreads (page 54). Look for glossy, bright, crisp, firm bell peppers rather than the soft, flimsy ones. You may refrigerate them in plastic bag for up to five days. This dish is traditionally made with green bell peppers, but you can use any color, and even mix them up. Bell peppers have vitamin A, which is responsible for beta-carotene that is good for your eyes. They also have vitamin C that acts as an antioxidant that helps your immune system.

Serves 3 to 4
Prep time: 10 minutes
Cook time: 20 minutes
Refrigerator Life: 3 days
Reheating Method: Place the refrigerated bell peppers and potatoes in a microwave and stir periodically. Or, place them in a skillet over medium-low heat and stir periodically.

2 green (or yellow, orange, red) bell peppers
1 medium russet potato (about ½ lb/225 g), peeled and diced into ¼ in (6 mm) cubes
1 small fully ripe tomato, such as plum (Roma), cut into 4 pieces
4 tablespoons vegetable oil
¾ teaspoon salt
1 teaspoon cumin seeds
¼ teaspoon ground turmeric
¼ teaspoon ground red pepper (cayenne)
¼ teaspoon ground black pepper

1 Wash the bell peppers. Cut off the stems and discard. Cut each bell pepper into 8 even lengthwise segments. Cut out any membranes and seeds and discard. Cut the bell pepper segments crosswise into ¼-inch (6 mm) thick slices.
2 Pour 2 tablespoons of the oil into a large nonstick skillet and place over medium heat. When the oil is heated, add the potato and ¼ teaspoon of the salt. Stir to combine. Cook, stirring frequently, until the potato is tender and you can easily insert a knife through the potato cubes, about 7 minutes. Some of the potato cubes may get lightly browned, which is okay. Turn off the heat and cover the skillet.
3 Pour the remaining 2 tablespoons of the oil into a medium saucepan and place over medium heat. When the oil is heated, add the tomato and cumin seeds. Stir to combine. Immediately add the bell peppers, turmeric, red pepper, black pepper, and the remaining ½ teaspoon of the salt. Stir to combine. Cook, stirring frequently, until the bell peppers are tender and you can easily insert a knife through them, about 10 minutes.
4 Add the potato cubes and stir to combine. Enjoy now or let cool to room temperature and refrigerate for later!

Mashed Turnips

Turnips might not be too popular of a vegetable, but fresh, sweet turnips cooked just right might make you a fan. Turnips are root vegetables that have a round shape with white skin and a purple top. The white flesh of turnips should be firm rather than soft or spongy. Smaller, young turnips are ideal, since they are still tender with a delicate, slightly sweet taste. Here we cook them into a tasty turnip mash (*shalgam ki subzi*), or they can be eaten raw in a salad, such as in my Fresh Lentil Sprout Salad (page 79). This dish can be served with Baked Whole Wheat Flatbreads (page 54). Turnips are a good source of calcium, which is good for overall bone strength and health.

Serves 3 to 4
Prep time: 10 minutes
Cook time: 35 minutes
Refrigerator Life: 3 days
Freezer Life: 1 month
Reheating Method: Place the refrigerated or defrosted turnips in a microwave and stir periodically. Or, place them in a skillet over medium-low heat and stir periodically.

6 small turnips (total 1½ lbs/700 g)
3 tablespoons vegetable oil
½ teaspoon ground turmeric
¼ teaspoon ground red pepper (cayenne)
½ teaspoon salt
¼ teaspoon ground black pepper
¼ cup (65 ml) water
1 tablespoon unsalted butter or vegan buttery spread

1 Wash the turnips. Cut off the tops and discard. Peel each turnip. Cut each turnip into 8 pieces. Taste a bite of the turnip to see if there are any sweet hints. If not, it is best to replace with another turnip.
2 Pour the oil into a medium saucepan and place over medium heat. When the oil is heated, add the turnips, turmeric, red pepper, salt, and black pepper. Stir to combine.
3 Reduce the heat to medium-low and cover the saucepan. Cook for 10 minutes, stirring occasionally.
4 Add the water. Cook covered until the turnips become completely soft and mashed, stirring occasionally and mashing the turnips with a large spoon, about 20 to 25 minutes.
5 Add the butter. Stir to combine until the butter is melted. Enjoy now or let cool to room temperature and refrigerate or freeze for later!

Sweet and Spicy Butternut Squash

It is amazing how this firm winter squash with its camel exterior and orange flesh easily cooks down into a soft mashed consistency. I made this dish at our family Thanksgiving dinner this year, and it was enjoyed by all. Butternut squash have thick necks with a rounded bottom. Look for firm ones with matte, rather than glossy skin, which indicate it was picked too early and will not be sweet. These squash keep for a few weeks in a cool dark place such as your pantry. Butternut squash have carotenoids, which are compounds that give it its bright orange color, help prevent cancer, and are good for your cardiovascular health.

Serves 3 to 4
Prep time: 10 minutes
Cook time: 25 minutes
Refrigerator life: 3 days
Freezer life: 1 month
Reheating method: Place the refrigerated or defrosted butternut squash in a microwave, cover and stir periodically. Or, place it in a saucepan over medium-low heat and stir periodically.

1 butternut squash (about 1½ lbs/700 g)
4 tablespoons vegetable oil
½ teaspoon cumin seeds
¼ teaspoon ground turmeric
¼ teaspoon ground red pepper (cayenne)
½ teaspoon salt
¼ teaspoon ground black pepper

1 Wash and peel the butternut squash with a vegetable peeler or knife. The peel is tough, so you may have to use a bit of force to peel it off until you see the orange-yellow flesh. Cut off both ends and discard. Cut the squash in half lengthwise. Scoop out any seeds and strings and discard. Chop the squash into about 1-inch (2.5 cm) pieces.
2 Pour the oil into a medium saucepan and place over medium heat. When the oil is heated, add the cumin seeds and let brown, about 10 seconds. Do not let the cumin seeds burn and turn black. Immediately add the chopped squash, turmeric, red pepper, salt, and black pepper. Stir to combine.
3 Reduce the heat to medium-low and cover the saucepan. Cook until the squash becomes completely soft and mashed, stirring occasionally and mashing the squash with a large spoon, about 25 minutes. Enjoy now or let cool to room temperature and refrigerate or freeze for later!

Curried Carrots and Peas

Carrot and pea curry (*gajar matar*) is an easy, delicious dish that is good for the health of your eyes. If you buy carrots with their leafy tops still on, tear them off to prevent the carrots from going limp and losing their nutrients more quickly. Carrots without their leafy tops will stay fresh for about one week stored in a plastic bag in the refrigerator's vegetable drawer. Avoid carrots that have splits or cracks, or that are limp. This dish has a nice saucy consistency to it, which makes it ideal to eat with Baked Whole Wheat Flatbreads (page 54), or with Plain Basmati Rice (page 63) or Rice with Cumin and Peas (page 64).

Serves 3 to 4
Prep time: 10 minutes
Cook time: 30 minutes
Refrigerator life: 3 days
Freezer life: 1 month
Reheating method: Place the refrigerated or defrosted curry in a microwave, cover and stir periodically. Or, place it in a saucepan over medium-low heat and stir periodically.

3 tablespoons vegetable oil
¼ teaspoon peeled and finely grated fresh ginger
½ small onion, shredded on the largest grating holes of a box grater
1 small fully ripe tomato, such as plum (Roma), cut into 4 pieces
¼ teaspoon ground turmeric
¼ teaspoon ground red pepper (cayenne)
½ teaspoon salt
½ teaspoon ground black pepper
3 medium carrots, peeled and sliced into thick matchsticks or ¼ in (6 mm) thick circles
1¼ cups (300 ml) water
1 cup (120 g) frozen or fresh green peas

1 Pour the oil into a medium saucepan and place over medium heat. When the oil is heated, add the ginger and onion. Sauté until the onion is golden brown, stirring frequently, about 5 minutes.
2 Reduce the heat to medium-low. Add the tomato. Cover the saucepan. Cook until the tomato becomes completely soft and mashed, and is combined with the onion to form a coarse paste, stirring every minute or so and lightly mashing the tomato, about 5 minutes.
3 Add the turmeric, red pepper, salt, and black pepper. Stir to combine. Cook uncovered for 6 minutes, stirring frequently.

4 Add the carrots and the water. Stir to combine. Bring to a rolling boil over high heat. Stir and reduce the heat to medium. Cover the saucepan. Simmer until the carrots are almost tender, stirring occasionally, about 6 minutes.
5 Add the peas. Cook uncovered for 5 minutes, stirring frequently. The water should be almost cooked off, leaving a saucy consistency. You should be able to easily insert a knife through the carrots. Enjoy now or let cool to room temperature and refrigerate or freeze for later.

1 lb (500 g) fresh green beans (American green beans or French haricot verts) or frozen, chopped or French cut green beans
3 tablespoons vegetable oil
1 teaspoon cumin seeds
1 medium russet potato (about ½ lb/ 225 g), peeled and diced into ¼ in (6 mm) cubes
½ teaspoon ground turmeric
¼ teaspoon ground red pepper (cayenne)
1 teaspoon salt
½ teaspoon ground black pepper

1 If you're using frozen green beans, do not defrost them. If you're using fresh green beans, wash them. Trim the tips and heads and discard. (If using haricot verts, only trim the head, and leave the the thin tip). Chop the green beans into ¼-inch (6 mm) pieces.
2 Pour the oil into a large nonstick skillet and place over medium heat. When the oil is heated, add the cumin seeds and let brown, about 10 seconds. Do not let the cumin seeds burn and turn black. Immediately add the green beans, turmeric, red pepper, salt, and black pepper. Stir thoroughly. Cover the skillet and cook for 5 minutes, stirring occasionally.
3 Remove the cover. Cook uncovered, stirring frequently, until the green beans are tender, and you can easily insert a knife through the potato cubes, about 20 minutes. Turn off the heat. Let rest, covered, for 5 minutes on the warm stove. Enjoy now or let cool to room temperature and refrigerate for later!

Green Beans with Potatoes

Green beans are deliciously nutritious, easy to grow, and popular in India. This easy to make green bean and potato sautéed dish (*aloo France beans*) goes best with Baked Whole Wheat Flatbreads (page 54). When shopping for fresh green beans, look for the bright green, crisp, and firm ones rather than the softer ones. The best ones will make a snapping noise when broken in half. You may refrigerate them in plastic bag for up to three days. Green beans are also called snap beans, French beans, and string beans. Green beans are a heart-healthy vegetable since they are a source of fiber.

Serves 3 to 4
Prep time: 5 minutes (15 minutes if using fresh green beans)
Cook time: 30 minutes
Refrigerator Life: 3 days
Freezer Life: 1 month
Reheating Method: Place the refrigerated or defrosted beans in a microwave and stir periodically. Or, place them in a skillet over medium-low heat and stir periodically.

Spinach and Potatoes

Although I really love palak *paneer* (*aka saag paner*), the creamed spinach and cheese cube Indian dish in my first book, I also love this spinach and potato dish (*aloo palak*) equally as well, and it is healthier! Spinach is excellent for you, as Popeye knows, it is a rich source of iron, which is a vital element for healthy muscles and red blood cells. When buying fresh spinach, look for dark green leaves free of bruises. If you are buying spinach in bunches instead of the bagged leaves, find ones which have firm, yet tender stems, they should not be lose and droopy or very tough. You may refrigerate them in plastic bag for up to three days. This dish goes best with the Baked Whole Wheat Flatbreads (page 54).

Serves 3 to 4
Prep time: 10 minutes
Cook time: 30 minutes
Refrigerator Life: 3 days
Freezer Life: 1 month
Reheating Method: Place the refrigerated or defrosted spinach and potatoes in a microwave and stir periodically. Or, place them in a skillet over medium-low heat and stir periodically.

1 lb (500 g) fresh spinach (about 2 bunches) or baby spinach
1 small fully ripe tomato, such as plum (Roma), cut into 4 pieces
¼ teaspoon ground turmeric
¼ teaspoon ground red pepper (cayenne)
¾ teaspoon salt
½ teaspoon ground black pepper
4 tablespoons vegetable oil
1 medium russet potato (about ½ lb/ 225 g), peeled and diced into ¼ in (6 mm) cubes
½ small onion, finely diced
1 teaspoon peeled and finely grated fresh ginger

1 Trim the bottom 1 inch (2.5 cm) off the stems of the spinach bunches and discard. Thoroughly wash the spinach. Coarsely chop the leaves and remaining stems. If using baby spinach, you do not need to trim the stems or chop the leaves. Squeeze the chopped spinach with your hands to remove any excess water.
2 Place the spinach, tomato, turmeric, red pepper, ½ teaspoon of the salt, and ¼ teaspoon of the black pepper in a medium saucepan set over medium heat.

You do not need to stir it right now. Cook for about 10 to15 minutes, stirring occasionally. You will soon see some water released from the spinach as it reduces in volume and becomes tender. Turn off the heat when the spinach is completely cooked down and you do not see any more water in the saucepan.
3 Using an immersion blender, purée the spinach and tomato until smooth, but do not liquefy it. (You can also use a regular blender, but be careful not to liquefy the spinach).
4 Pour 2 tablespoons of the oil into a large nonstick skillet and place over medium heat. When the oil is heated, add the potato and the remaining ¼ teaspoon each of the salt and black pepper. Stir to combine. Cook, stirring frequently, until the potato is tender and you can easily insert a knife through the potato cubes, about 7 minutes. Some of the potato cubes may get lightly browned, which is okay. Turn off the heat. Let rest, covered, for 5 minutes on the warm stove.
5 Add the potato cubes into the saucepan with the blended spinach and stir to combine.
6 Pour the remaining 2 tablespoons of oil into the empty skillet. When the oil is heated, add the onion and ginger. Sauté until the onion is golden brown, stirring frequently, about 5 minutes. Pour into the saucepan with the potato cubes and blended spinach and stir to combine. Enjoy now or let cool to room temperature and refrigerate or freeze for later!

Cauliflower and Potatoes

India is one of the top producers of cauliflower, so it's no wonder that this dish (*aloo gobi*) is very popular in Indian cuisine. It is usually eaten with the Baked Whole Wheat Flatbreads (page 54). When selecting fresh cauliflower heads, look for ones that are firm and creamy white, without any brown markings. My mom sometimes makes "Indian burritos" for my dad's lunch by rolling some of this dish in a *chapati*. It tastes great at room temperature without needing to reheat it in the microwave and filling the office with the aroma of Indian spices! Pregnant women benefit from cauliflower since it is rich in folate and vitamin C. Folate helps proper development of the baby and vitamin C keeps your immune system healthy.

Serves 3 to 4
Prep time: 5 minutes (10 minutes if using fresh head of cauliflower)
Cook time: 30 minutes
Refrigerator Life: 3 days
Freezer Life: 1 month
Reheating Method: Place the refrigerated or defrosted cauliflower in a microwave and stir periodically. Or, place it in a skillet over medium-low heat and stir periodically.

1 large head fresh cauliflower (about 2 lbs/1 kg) or 1 lb (500 g) frozen bite-size cauliflower florets
3 tablespoons vegetable oil
1 fully ripe tomato, cut into 4 pieces
1 medium russet potato (about ½ lb/225 g), peeled and cut into ½ in (1.25 cm) cubes
2 teaspoons peeled and finely grated fresh ginger
1 teaspoon cumin seeds
½ teaspoon ground turmeric
¼ teaspoon ground red pepper (cayenne)
1¼ teaspoons salt
¼ teaspoon ground black pepper
1 handful fresh coriander leaves(cilantro) (about ¼ cup/10 g packed leaves), rinsed and chopped

1 If you're using frozen cauliflower, do not defrost. If you're using fresh cauliflower, cut the florets off the cauliflower head into large bite-size pieces and wash with cold water. (See page 23 for how to cut fresh cauliflower)

2 Pour the oil into a large nonstick skillet and place over medium heat. When the oil is heated, add the tomato. Cover the skillet. Cook until the tomato becomes soft and mashed, stirring every minute or so and lightly mashing the tomato, about 5 minutes.

3 Add the cauliflower, potato, ginger, cumin seeds, turmeric, red pepper, salt, and black pepper. Stir to combine until everything is stained yellow from the turmeric. Increase the heat to medium-high. Cook covered for 7 minutes, stirring occasionally.

4 Reduce the heat to medium. Remove the cover to avoid letting the cauliflower become mushy. Cook until the cauliflower is tender and you can easily insert a knife through the potato cubes, stirring occasionally, about 10 minutes. You may sprinkle some water in the skillet if you feel the cauliflower is drying up while the potatoes are cooking.

5 Turn off the heat. Cover for 5 minutes on the warm stove. Enjoy now or let cool to room temperature and refrigerate or freeze for later! Just before serving, sprinkle the chopped coriander leaves on top.

Sautéed Mushrooms and Peas

Mushrooms are my favorite vegetable and I am excited that is seems to be one of my daughter's favorite vegetables as well. When my dad was a child in India, his father would occasionally go to the city to buy a variety of mushrooms, where they are considered a delicacy since they were not commonly available and were expensive. Fresh mushrooms tend to have a lot of dirt since they grow close to the ground, and so I am very particular about giving them a quick rinse. Look for firm, evenly colored mushrooms with tightly closed caps. This dish, called *khumb matar*, can be eaten with the Baked Whole Wheat Flatbreads (page 54). Mushrooms are a good source of potassium.

Serves 3 to 4
Prep time: 10 minutes
Cook time: 30 minutes
Refrigerator Life: 3 days
Freezer Life: 1 month
Reheating Method: Place the refrigerated or defrosted mushrooms and peas in a microwave and stir periodically. Or, place them in a skillet over medium-low heat and stir periodically.

½ lb (225 g) fresh whole or pre-sliced
    mushrooms
3 tablespoons vegetable oil
½ small onion, shredded on the largest
    grating holes of a box grater
1 fully ripe tomato, cut into 4 pieces
¼ teaspoon ground turmeric
¼ teaspoon ground red pepper (cayenne)
½ teaspoon salt
½ teaspoon ground black pepper
½ cup (60 g) frozen or fresh green peas

1 If you are using whole mushrooms, clean them by placing them in a colander and running cold water on them while using your fingers or a mushroom brush to gently rub away any dirt. Cut the cleaned mushrooms into ¼-inch (6 mm) or thinner longitudinal slices.
2 Pour the oil into a medium saucepan and place over medium heat. When the oil is heated, add the onion. Sauté until the onion is golden brown, stirring frequently, about 5 minutes.
3 Reduce the heat to medium-low and add the tomato. Cover the saucepan. Cook until the tomato becomes completely soft and mashed and is combined with the onion to form a coarse paste, stirring every minute or so and lightly mashing the tomato, about 5 minutes.

4 Add the turmeric, red pepper, salt, and black pepper. Stir to combine. Cook uncovered for 6 minutes, stirring frequently.
5 Add the mushrooms. Stir to combine. Increase the heat to medium and cover the saucepan. Cook 5 minutes, stirring occasionally. The mushrooms will begin to reduce in volume as they release their water.
6 Remove the cover. Cook 5 minutes, stirring frequently. The water that was released by the mushrooms will almost all cook off.
7 Add the peas. Cook uncovered for 5 minutes, stirring frequently. Enjoy now or let cool to room temperature and refrigerate or freeze for later!

Sautéed Potatoes with Cumin

Potatoes are such simple and humble tuber vegetables, yet bring so much to the table. In this easy and delicious potato dish, I boil potatoes and then sauté them with cumin seeds. My daughter enjoys this potato dish, and I like to pack it in her lunch, along with a small baby fork that she uses to prick each potato cube and eat it. This dish can be eaten with the Baked Whole Wheat Flatbreads (page 54), or even pressed between two slices of toast for a unique and tasty sandwich. Potatoes should be firm and without wrinkles or sprouts. You can store them in a cool pantry or your refrigerator for about one week. Potatoes are rich in Vitamin B6, which helps maintain healthy brain and nerve function, and is needed for cellular renewal, a healthy nervous system, and a balanced mood.

Serves 3 to 4
Prep time: 35 minutes to boil the potatoes (can be done 1 day in advance)
Cook time: 5 minutes
Refrigerator Life: 3 days
Freezer Life: 1 month
Reheating Method: Place the refrigerated or defrosted potatoes in a microwave and stir periodically. Or, place it in a skillet over medium-low heat and stir periodically.

2 medium russet potatoes (total 1 lb/500 g), boiled (see page 22)
4 tablespoons vegetable oil
1 teaspoon cumin seeds
¼ teaspoon ground turmeric
¼ teaspoon ground red pepper (cayenne)
½ heaping teaspoon salt
½ teaspoon ground black pepper
Juice of ½ lime

1 Peel the boiled potatoes and cut into ¾-inch (2 cm) cubes.
2 Pour the oil into a medium saucepan and place over medium heat. When the oil is heated, add the cumin seeds and let brown, about 10 seconds. Do not let the cumin seeds burn and turn black. Immediately add the cubed potatoes, turmeric, red pepper, salt, and black pepper. Stir to combine.
3 Reduce the heat to medium-low. Cook for 5 minutes, stirring frequently. If any potatoes or spices start sticking to the bottom of the pan, scrape it and stir it in as this improves the flavor. The potato cubes may get a bit mushy and lose their shape, which is okay. Turn off the heat.
4 Add the lime juice. Stir to combine. Enjoy now or let cool to room temperature and refrigerate or freeze for later!

Yellow Squash Curry

Yellow squash is a summer squash with a mildly sweet and tender flesh and thin yellow skin. A good yellow summer squash will be small, firm, and have tender skin free of blemishes and bruising. It should be kept in a plastic bag in the refrigerator for no more than five days. Since this dish has a curry consistency, it can be served with Plain Basmati Rice (page 63) or Rice with Cumin and Peas (page 64), but this dish is also can be eaten with Baked Whole Wheat Flatbreads (page 54). Yellow squash has beta carotene and lutein, which are important for good eye health. It also has vitamin C and manganese, which promote healthy bones.

Serves 3 to 4
Prep time: 5 minutes
Cook time: 25 minutes
Refrigerator Life: 3 days
Freezer Life: 1 month
Reheating Method: Place the refrigerated or defrosted squash in a microwave and stir periodically. Or, place it in a skillet over medium-low heat and stir periodically.

3 small yellow squash (total 1 lb/500 g)
3 tablespoons vegetable oil
½ small onion, shredded on the largest
    grating holes of a box grater
1 small fully ripe tomato, such as plum
    (Roma), cut into 4 pieces
½ teaspoon cumin seeds
¼ teaspoon ground turmeric
¼ teaspoon ground red pepper (cayenne)
¾ teaspoon salt
¼ teaspoon ground black pepper
1 cup (250 ml) water

1 Wash the squash. Cut off both ends and discard. Slice into thin circles, about ¼-inch (6 mm) thick.
2 Pour the oil into a medium saucepan and place over medium heat. When the oil is heated, add the onion. Sauté until the onion is golden brown, stirring frequently, about 5 minutes.
3 Reduce the heat to medium-low and add the tomato. Cover the saucepan and cook until the tomato becomes completely soft and mashed and is combined with the onion to form a coarse paste, stirring every minute or so and lightly mashing the tomato, about 5 minutes.
4 Add the cumin seeds, turmeric, red pepper, salt, and black pepper. Stir to combine. Cook uncovered for 3 minutes, stirring frequently.
5 Add the squash. Stir to combine. Cook for 2 minutes, stirring frequently.
6 Add the water. Bring to a rolling boil over high heat. Stir and reduce the heat to medium-low. Simmer until the squash is tender, stirring occasionally, about 10 minutes. Some of the water will cook off, but the dish will still have a curry base. Enjoy now or let cool to room temperature and refrigerate or freeze for later!

Stuffed Okra

Okra, known as "lady's fingers" in India, has a beautiful, bright green color and a wonderful taste. When buying okra look for crisp ones in which the tail end can be snapped off and avoid the flimsy ones with black markings. My mother has tall stalks of okra plants every summer in her garden, and my daughter plucks them and eats them raw! In this okra dish, whole okra are stuffed with spices and then cooked with onions. This dish goes best with Baked Whole Wheat Flatbreads (page 54) and served with a lentil dish of your choice. Okra is high in fiber, which means it is good for our digestive tract. Okra can be refrigerated in a plastic bag for up to three days.

Serves 3 to 4
Prep time: 15 minutes
Cook time: 20 minutes
Refrigerator Life: 3 days
Freezer Life: 1 month
Reheating Method: Place the refrigerated or defrosted okra in a microwave, cover and turn periodically. Or, place it in a saucepan over medium-low heat and turn periodically.

1 lb (500 g) fresh okra
6 tablespoons vegetable oil
1 small onion, thickly sliced into half-moons

SPICE STUFFING
2¾ teaspoons ground turmeric
1¼ teaspoons ground red pepper (cayenne)
1¾ teaspoons salt
2¾ teaspoons ground black pepper

1 Wash the okra. Trim the tips and heads and discard. Using a small knife, slice into each okra lengthwise down the middle as deep as possible, making sure not to cut the okra in half.
2 Place the ingredients for the Spice Stuffing in a small bowl. Mix well. Hold an okra in one hand and gently pry it open. Evenly drizzle about ¼ teaspoon of the Spice Stuffing into each okra.
3 Pour 5 tablespoons of the oil into a large nonstick skillet and place over medium heat. When the oil is heated, add the stuffed okra. Spread out the okra in the skillet. Cook for 10 minutes, turning the okra every few minutes. The okra will start to become tender and the skins will start to brown.
4 Reduce the heat to medium-low. Cover the skillet and cook until the okra is tender, turning the okra occasionally, about 5 minutes.
5 Remove the cooked okra from the skillet and place in a serving dish.
6 Add the remaining tablespoon of oil and the onion to the skillet. Cook on medium-low until the onion is just tender and a bit crisp, stirring frequently, about 5 minutes. Remove the onion from the skillet and mix it with the okra. Enjoy now or let it cool and freeze for later!

How to Stuff the Okra

FIRST When slicing into an okra, make sure not to cut the okra completely in half. **SECOND** Here you can see the okra sliced deeply lengthwise.

THIRD Stuff the okra with the Spice Stuffing. **FOURTH** Here is the Stuffed Okra ready to cook in a skillet.

Fenugreek and Potatoes

Fresh fenugreek leaves tend to be a bit bitter, but when cooked with potatoes, the flavors are balanced out to create this tasty dish. Look for bright green fenugreek bunches that are not wilted. Like other leafy greens, fenugreek is a good source of fiber.

Serves 2 to 3
Prep time: 10 minutes
Cook time: 20 minutes
Refrigerator Life: 3 days
Freezer Life: 1 month
Reheating Method: Place the refrigerated or defrosted fenugreek and potatoes in a microwave and stir periodically. Or, place them in a skillet over medium-low heat and stir periodically.

½ lb (225 g) fresh fenugreek (about 1 bunch)
¼ teaspoon ground turmeric
¼ teaspoon ground red pepper (cayenne)
¼ teaspoon ground black pepper
½ teaspoon salt
2 tablespoons vegetable oil
1 medium russet potato (about ½ lb/ 225 g), peeled and cut into ¼-inch (6-mm) cubes

1 Cut off the stems at the bottom of the fenugreek bunch where the leafy part ends and discard. The stems at the bottom of the bunch are not tender like the leafy upper stems. Thoroughly wash the fenugreek. Finely chop the leaves and remaining stems. Squeeze the chopped fenugreek with your hands to remove any excess water.

2 Place the fenugreek, turmeric, red pepper, black pepper, and ¼ teaspoon of the salt in a medium saucepan set over medium heat. You do not need to stir it right now. Cook for about 8 minutes, stirring occasionally. There will be a distinct aroma of fenugreek as it cooks. You will soon see a bit of water released from the fenugreek as it reduces in volume and becomes tender. Turn off the heat when the fenugreek is completely cooked down and you do not see any more water in the saucepan.

3 Pour the oil into a large nonstick skillet and place over medium heat. When the oil is heated add the potato and the remaining ¼ teaspoon of the salt. Stir to combine. Cook, stirring frequently, until the potato is tender and you can easily insert a knife through the potato cubes, about 7 minutes. Some of the potato cubes may get lightly browned, which is okay. Turn off the heat. Let rest, covered, for 5 minutes on the warm stove.

4 Add the potato cubes into the saucepan with the fenugreek and stir to combine. Enjoy now or let cool to room temperature and refrigerate or freeze for later!

Stuffed Bitter Melon

Bitter melons aren't for everyone, but my daughter enjoys eating them. Look for Indian bitter melon, which is smaller and has pointed ends as compared to the bigger, oblong Chinese variety. Bitter melon has been shown to help lower blood sugar level, decrease cholesterol levels, and cleans and detoxifies the blood.

Serves 3 to 4
Prep time: 15 minutes + overnight sitting (12 hours)
Cook time: 30 minutes
Refrigerator Life: 3 days
Reheating Method: Place the refrigerated bitter melon and onions in a microwave, cover and stir periodically. Or, place it in a skillet over medium-low heat and stir periodically.

4 medium bitter melons (total ½ lb/225 g)
2¼ teaspoons salt
2 small onions
Juice of 1 lime
½ teaspoon ground turmeric
¼ teaspoon ground red pepper (cayenne)
½ teaspoon ground black pepper
4½ tablespoons vegetable oil

How to Stuff the Bitter Melon

FIRST Cut off the top end of the bitter melon. **SECOND** Scrape off the bitter melon's bumpy skin.

THIRD Slit open the bitter melon. **FOURTH** Very hard and ripe seeds removed. You may leave in any soft, tender seeds with their tender casings. **FIFTH** Salt rubbed all around the outside and inside of each bitter melon.

1 Cut off the top ends of each bitter melon and discard. Leave the tail-ends on for presentation. Scrape the bumpy skin off each bitter melon by holding it in one hand and using a small knife to scrape it until is smooth. Rinse the scraped bitter melons.

2 Using a small knife, slit each bitter melon lengthwise without cutting it in half. Pry it open with your hands and feel around for the seeds. Remove any very hard and ripe seeds and discard. You can leave the tender and soft seeds inside along with their tender casings.

3 Rub ½ teaspoon of salt around the outside and inside of the bitter melon to draw out the bitterness. Place the bitter melons on a plate and cover. Refrigerate overnight.

4 The next day, rinse the inside and outside of each bitter melon with water. Gently squeeze out the water of each melon with one hand.

5 Grate one onion on the largest grating holes of a box grater and place in a small bowl.

6 Add the lime juice, turmeric, red pepper, black pepper, and the remaining ¼ teaspoon of the salt. Stir to combine. Divide the mixture into 4 equal parts. Using a small spoon or your fingers, evenly stuff each bitter melon with the mixture.

7 Pour 4 tablespoons of the oil into a medium nonstick skillet and place over medium heat. When the oil is heated, add the bitter melons, slit side up. Cook for 2 minutes and then turn the bitter melons. They should be light brown on the cooked side

8 Cook for 2 minutes and turn again. The bitter melons should start to turn brown.

9 Cook for 2 minutes and turn again. Reduce the heat to low. Cover the skillet. Continue to cook the bitter melons, turning every few minutes, for about 15 minutes, or until they are tender and you can easily poke a knife through the skin. The bitter melons should be brownish with some darker marks.Turn off the heat and remove the bitter melons from the skillet.

10 Cut the remaining onion into thickly sliced half moons. Add the remaining ½ tablespoon of the oil to the skillet and place over medium heat. When the oil is heated, add the onion. Slightly cook until the onion is just a bit tender and still a bit crisp, stirring frequently, about 5 minutes. Remove the onion from the skillet and place on a serving platter. Add the cooked bitter melons on top of the onions. Enjoy now or let cool to room temperature and refrigerate for later.

Opo Squash Dumpling Curry

This dish has a nice saucy consistency to it, which makes it ideal to eat with Rice with Cumin and Peas (page 64), or even with Baked Whole Wheat Flatbreads (page 54).

Serves 2 to 3
Prep time: 10 minutes + 20 minutes to make the Opo Squash Fritters
Cook time: 25 minutes
Refrigerator Life: 3 days
Reheating Method: Place the refrigerated curry in a microwave, cover and stir periodically. Or, place it in a saucepan over medium-low heat and stir periodically.

1 recipe (Opo Squash Fritters) plus the ½ cup (125 ml) squeezed squash water
3 tablespoons vegetable oil
½ small onion, shredded on the largest grating holes of a box grater
1 fully ripe tomato, cut into 4 pieces
¼ teaspoon ground turmeric
¼ teaspoon ground red pepper (cayenne)
2 pinches salt
½ teaspoon ground black pepper
½ cup (125 ml) water

1 Pour the oil into a medium saucepan and place over medium heat. When the oil is heated, add the onion. Sauté until the onion is golden brown, stirring frequently, about 5 minutes.

2 Reduce the heat to medium-low and add the tomato. Cover the saucepan. Cook until the tomato becomes completely soft and mashed and is combined with the onion to form a coarse paste, stirring every minute or so and lightly mashing the tomato, about 5 minutes.

3 Add the turmeric, red pepper, salt, and black pepper. Stir to combine. Cook uncovered for 6 minutes, stirring frequently.

4 Add the ½ cup (125 ml) squeezed squash water that was saved when making the Opo Squash Fritters. Add ½ cup (125 ml) plain water. Bring to rolling boil over high heat. Turn off the heat.

5 Add the Opo Squash Fritters. Let rest, covered, for 5 minutes on the warm stove, stirring once in between. Enjoy now or let cool to room temperature and refrigerate for later!

Japanese Eggplants with Potatoes

Eggplants, also known as *brinjal* in India and "aubergine" in Europe, come in different shapes, varieties and colors from white to green to purples. In America, the most common is the big, thicker skinned globe eggplant. The light purple Chinese eggplant and dark purple Japanese eggplant are narrower and have a more delicate, somewhat sweet flavor than the globe. The Chinese, Japanese, and small round Indian eggplants have a smooth, thin, glossy skin that is not necessary to peel. When buying an eggplant, pick out ones that are not too firm, and not too soft, but tender to the touch, and that do not have brown spots or discoloration on the skin. Here I use the easily available Japanese eggplants with potatoes to make this delicious dish. Studies have shown that eggplants lower high cholesterol levels that can damage arteries and cause heart disease.

Serves 3 to 4
Prep time: 10 minutes
Cook time: 40 minutes
Refrigerator Life: 3 days
Reheating Method: Place the refrigerated eggplants and potatoes in a microwave, cover and stir periodically. Or, place it in a skillet over medium-low heat and stir periodically.

2 Japanese or Chinese eggplants (total ½ lb/225 g)
1 medium russet potato (about ½ lb/225 g)
6 tablespoons vegetable oil
1 small onion, shredded on the largest grating holes of a box grater
1 small fully ripe tomato, such as plum (Roma), cut into 4 pieces
¼ teaspoon ground turmeric
½ teaspoon ground red pepper (cayenne)
¾ teaspoon salt
¾ teaspoon ground black pepper

1 Wash the eggplants. Do not peel them. Cut each eggplant in half crosswise. Cut each half lengthwise into 4 even segments, leaving the stem on and cutting through it as well. Fill a large bowl with water. Place the cut eggplant pieces into the bowl of water to prevent browning.
2 Wash and peel the potato. Cut the potato in half lengthwise. Slice each half

lengthwise into ½-inch (1.25 cm) thick wedges. The potato wedges should be similar in size to the eggplant pieces. Place the potato wedges into another bowl of water to prevent browning.

3 Pour 5 tablespoons of the oil into a large nonstick skillet and place over medium heat. When the oil is heated, add the onion. Sauté until the onion is golden brown, stirring frequently, about 5 minutes.

4 Reduce the heat to medium-low and add the tomato. Cover the saucepan. Cook until the tomato becomes completely soft and mashed and is combined with the onion to form a coarse paste, stirring every minute or so and lightly mashing the tomato, about 5 minutes.

5 Add ¼ teaspoon each of the turmeric and red pepper and ½ teaspoon each of the salt and black pepper. Stir to combine. Cook uncovered for 6 minutes, stirring frequently.

6 Drain the water from the eggplant and add the eggplant to the skillet. Sit to combine. Increase the heat to medium. Cook until the eggplant is tender and you can easily insert a knife through it, stirring occasionally, about 8 minutes. Remove the eggplant from the skillet and place on a plate.

7 Pour the remaining tablespoon of the oil into the skillet and place over medium heat. When the oil is heated, drain the water from the potato and add the potato and the remaining ¼ teaspoon each of the red pepper, salt, and black pepper. Stir to combine. Cook, stirring frequently, until the potato is tender and you can easily insert a knife through the potato wedges, about 10 minutes. Turn off the heat.

8 Add the eggplant back to the skillet. Gently mix to combine with the potato wedges. Let rest, covered, for 5 minutes on the warm stove. Enjoy now or let cool to room temperature and refrigerate for later!

Cabbage and Peas

Cabbage is best when it has sweet undertones. Although cabbage may vary in color from green to reddish-purple, this dish is traditionally made with green cabbage. Look for compact heads of waxy, tightly wrapped leaves that are crisp and firmly packed. Cabbage is a good source of vitamin C, making it rich in antioxidants.

Serves 4
Prep time: 10 minutes
Cook time: 20 minutes
Refrigerator Life: 3 days
Reheating Method: Place the refrigerated cabbage and peas in a microwave and stir periodically. Or, place them in a skillet over medium-low heat and stir periodically.

1 small head fresh green cabbage (about 2 lbs/1 kg)
4 tablespoons vegetable oil
½ teaspoon ground turmeric
¼ teaspoon ground red pepper (cayenne)
1 teaspoon salt
½ teaspoon ground black pepper
1 cup (120 g) frozen or fresh green peas

1 Pull away the outer layer of leaves from the cabbage head and discard. Using a bit of force, cut the cabbage into 4 even segments through the stem. Cut out the tough bottom core in each segment and discard. Working with one segment at a time, cut it crosswise into thin ⅛-inch (3 mm) slices. The slices will fall apart into thin shreds.

2 Pour the oil into a large saucepan and place over medium heat. When the oil is heated, add the shredded cabbage, turmeric, red pepper, salt, and black pepper. Cook for 15 minutes, stirring occasionally. The cabbage will start to reduce in volume.

3 Add the peas. Stir to combine. Cook until the cabbage is tender, stirring occasionally, about 5 minutes. Enjoy now or let cool to room temperature and refrigerate for later.

Mixed Greens

In the cooler months when mustard greens and spinach are in season, they are cooked together and served with Indian Cornbread (page 61).

Serves 2 to 3
Prep time: 15 minutes
Cook time: 1 hour
Refrigerator Life: 3 days
Freezer Life: 1 month
Reheating Method: Place the refrigerated or defrosted mixed greens in a microwave and stir periodically. Or, place them in a saucepan over medium-low heat and stir periodically.

½ lb (225 g) fresh mustard greens (1 small bunch)
½ lb (225 g) fresh turnip greens (1 small bunch) or mustard greens again
½ lb (225 g) fresh spinach (1 bunch) or baby spinach
1 fully ripe tomato, cut into 4 pieces
½ teaspoon ground red pepper (cayenne)

¾ teaspoon salt
2 tablespoons vegetable oil
2 tablespoons peeled and finely grated fresh ginger
1 fresh finger-length green chili pepper, sliced into thin circles (any variety)
2 tablespoons unsalted butter or vegan buttery spread

1 Thoroughly wash the mustard greens Trim the bottom ¼ inch (6 mm) off the stems and discard. Stack a few stalks of mustard greens together and cut them, starting from the stem end, crosswise into ¼-inch (6 mm) pieces. When you get to the leafy part, bunch the leaves together and keep cutting into ¼-inch (6 mm) pieces.

2 Thoroughly wash and cut the turnip greens the same way as the mustard greens.

3 Trim the bottom 1 inch (2.5 cm) off the stems of the spinach bunch and discard. Thoroughly wash the spinach. Coarsely chop the leaves and remaining stems. If using baby spinach, you do not need to trim the stems or chop the leaves.

4 Squeeze the chopped greens and stems with your hands to remove any excess water and place them in a large saucepan over medium heat. Add the tomato and cook for 10 minutes. You will soon see some water released from the greens as they start to reduce in volume.

5 Add the red pepper and salt. Stir to combine and cover. Cook for about 40 to 45 minutes so the greens completely cook down and become tender, stirring occasionally. Turn off the heat when you do not see any more water in the saucepan.

6 Transfer the cooked greens and stems to a blender. Purée until smooth, but do not liquefy it, and then put the puréed contents back in the saucepan.

7 Pour the oil into a small skillet and place over medium heat. When the oil is heated, add the ginger and green chili pepper. Sauté for 3 minutes, stirring frequently. Pour into the saucepan with the blended greens.

8 Add the butter. Stir to combine until the butter is melted. Enjoy now or let cool to room temperature and refrigerate or freeze for later!

Collard Greens and Parsnips

Collard greens are popular in the southern US states, and are a staple of soul food. When collard greens and parsnips are cooked using Indian cooking techniques and flavors, the result is amazing and goes well with Baked Whole Wheat Flatbreads (page 54).

Serves 3 to 4
Prep time: 15 minutes
Cook time: 25 minutes
Refrigerator Life: 3 days
Freezer Life: 1 month
Reheating Method: Place the refrigerated or defrosted collard greens and parsnips in a microwave and stir periodically. Or, place them in a skillet over medium-low heat and stir periodically.

½ lb (225 g) fresh collard greens
   (about 1 small bunch)
2 small parsnips (about ½ lb/225 g)
¼ teaspoon ground turmeric
½ teaspoon ground red pepper (cayenne)
½ teaspoon ground black pepper
¾ teaspoon salt
2½ tablespoons vegetable oil

1 Thoroughly wash the collard greens. To de-rib (separating the leaves from the stem) the collard greens, working with one stem of greens at a time, cut around the stem in a v-shape. Tightly roll up the leafy greens and then slice the roll crosswise into thin strips, about ¼-inch (6 mm) thick. Coarsely chop up the strips.

2 Trim the bottom ¼ inch (6 mm) off the stems and discard. Cut the stems into about ¼-inch (6 mm) small pieces.

3 Peel and wash the parsnips. Cut off both ends and discard. Cut the parsnips into four equal lengthwise segments. Cut each segment crosswise into ¼-inch (6 mm) pieces.

4 Squeeze the chopped greens with your hands to remove any excess water. Place the collard greens, chopped stems, turmeric, ¼ teaspoon each of the red pepper and the black pepper, and ½ teaspoon of the salt into a medium saucepan set over medium heat. You do not need to stir it right now. Cook covered for about 8 minutes, stirring occasionally. You will soon see some water released from the greens as they start to reduce in volume and become tender. Turn off the heat when the greens are completely cooked down and you do not see any more water in the saucepan.

5 Pour the oil into a large nonstick skillet and place over medium heat. When the oil is heated, add the parsnips. Add the remaining ¼ teaspoon each of the red pepper, black pepper, and salt. Stir to combine. Cook, stirring frequently, until the parsnips are tender and you can easily insert a knife through the pieces, about 8 minutes. Turn off the heat. Let rest, covered, for 5 minutes on the warm stove.

6 Add the parsnip pieces into the saucepan with the collard greens and stir to combine. Enjoy now or let cool to room temperature and refrigerate or freeze for later!

CHAPTER 6

Tofu and Cheese

Tofu and *paneer*, the famous Indian homemade cheese, may be used interchangeably to create healthy, delicious, and protein-rich dishes. Firm tofu and *paneer* have similar textures and soak up the flavor of the surrounding spices. Tofu, also called bean curd, is made from curdled soymilk, which is the iron-rich liquid extracted from cooked soybeans. The texture of tofu, ranging from silky-smooth to extra firm, depends on how the soymilk is processed. I use firm tofu in my recipes due to its similarity to *paneer* in texture. *Paneer* also has different textures depending on how much of the water is pressed out of it. Both tofu and *paneer* can be cooked in different ways, such as crumbling them to make a Tofu Breakfast Scramble (page 111), grilling them to make Tandoori Tofu Kebabs (page 113), sautéeing them to make Cheese and Bell Pepper Skewers (page 108), and cubing and pan-frying them to make Creamed Swiss Chard with Cheese Cubes (page 107) and mouth-watering curries such as Indian Cheese and Pea Curry (page 106).

Tofu and *paneer* both have protein, which is good for muscle building and repair for the body. Tofu is also easy to digest, low in calories and sodium, cholesterol free, and a good source of iron, which is needed for oxygen transport in our body. Tofu is considered a complete protein, meaning it has the nine essential amino acids the body needs to build the proteins that help maintain muscle, bone, and organs. Not all of these nine amino acids are generated by our bodies, but animal food sources such as meat and fish do have them all. Tofu and quinoa are the plant-based exceptions that have all nine amino acids. *Paneer* is made from whole cow's or buffalo's milk instead of soymilk, making it a bit higher in fat and calories as compared to tofu, but gives it a good amount of calcium.

If you are not a fan of tofu yet, I encourage you to try my easy tofu recipes and you just might enjoy cooking with it as much as the *paneer* dishes!

Homemade Crumbled Indian Cheese *Paneer*

Paneer is the Hindi word for cheese, and this soft Indian cheese is the crumbled, un-pressed form of the Indian Cheese Block (page 105). It is made from boiling milk that is separated into curds and whey by introducing lime juice. The whey is drained, leaving fresh homemade cheese that is used to make the scrumptious Crumbled Indian Cheese with Peas (page 112). It is best to use whole milk instead of reduced fat milk when making this cheese to get the most yield and a creamier taste and texture. You may use a firm tofu block and crumble it as a substitute.

Makes 1 cup (135 g)
Prep work: 5 minutes
Cook time: 5 minutes
Refrigerator life: 1 day
Reheating method: None! Simply use to make desired dish.

4 cups (1 liter) whole milk
Juice of 1 lime

How to Make the Homemade Crumbled Indian Cheese

FIRST Bring the milk to a rolling boil. **SECOND** Add the lime juice to the boiling milk. **THIRD** Curdled milk will separate into curds (solid cheese clumps) and whey (watery liquid).

FOURTH Pouring the curdled milk into a cheesecloth lined colander to collect the curds and drain the whey. **FIFTH** Gather up the sides of the cheesecloth to create a bundle after the whey has drained. **SIXTH** Use the back of a spoon to squeeze out the excess whey from the bundle of cheese.

1 Pour the milk into a heavy bottomed, medium-sized stockpot. Slowly bring to a rolling boil over medium-high heat, stirring frequently as it comes to a boil. Don't let the milk boil over and out of the pot! Immediately turn off the heat.
2 Add the lime juice and gently stir for about 45 seconds, or until the milk separates into curds (solid cheese clumps) and whey (watery liquid). (If the milk does not separate, add more lime juice—2 teaspoons at a time—until it does.) The whey may appear to be light green in color from the lime juice. Turn off the heat.
3 Fold a large piece of cheesecloth into 4 layers (this will keep the cheese from falling through). Line a colander with the folded cheesecloth and place it over a large bowl to catch the whey. Gently pour the separated milk into the cheesecloth-lined colander. Let the whey drain through the colander down into the sink.
4 When the whey has stopped draining (about 1 minute), gather up the sides of the cheesecloth to create a bundle. Using the back of a spoon, gently press the bundle against the side of the colander to squeeze out most of the excess whey. It is okay if the cheese is somewhat moist. Be careful, as it will be hot.
5 Remove the cheese from the cheesecloth and place in a small bowl. The *paneer* is now ready to be used to make Indian Cheese with Peas (page 112), or it may be placed in an airtight container and refrigerated up to 1 day before using.

Vegetable Curry with Tofu

My daughter and I enjoy this dish with Rice with Cumin and Peas (page 64). Coconut milk has many health benefits and tastes amazing!

Serves 3 to 4
Prep time: 15 minutes + 20 minutes sitting + 10 minutes to pan-fry the tofu
Cook time: 25 minutes
Refrigerator life: 3 days
Freezer life: 1 month
Reheating method: Place the refrigerated or defrosted curry in a microwave, cover and stir periodically. Or, place it in a saucepan over medium-low heat and stir periodically.

2 tablespoons vegetable oil
2 teaspoons minced garlic
1 teaspoon peeled and finely grated fresh ginger
1 fully ripe tomato, cut into 4 pieces
½ teaspoon ground turmeric
¼ teaspoon ground red pepper (cayenne)
½ teaspoon salt
1 teaspoon store bought or Garam Masala (page 109)
½ small onion, thinly sliced into half-moons
1 cup (120 g) frozen or fresh green peas
1 medium russet potato (about ½ lb/225 g), peeled and cut into ½ in (1.25 cm) cubes
1 carrot, peeled and cut into thin or thick matchsticks
½ block firm tofu (about ½ lb/225 g), cubed and pan-fried (page 110)
1 cup (250 ml) coconut milk
¼ cup (65 ml) water

1 Pour the oil into a medium saucepan and place over medium heat. When the oil is heated, add the garlic and ginger. Sauté until the garlic is lightly browned, stirring frequently, about 30 seconds.
2 Reduce the heat to medium-low and add the tomato. Cover the saucepan and cook until the tomato becomes completely soft and mashed, stirring every minute or so and lightly mashing the tomato, about 5 minutes.
3 Add the turmeric, red pepper, salt, and Garam Masala. Stir to combine. Cook uncovered for 2 minutes, stirring frequently.
4 Add the onion, peas, potato, carrot, pan-fried tofu, coconut milk, and water. Stir to combine. Bring to a rolling boil over high heat.
5 Reduce the heat to medium-low and cover the saucepan. Simmer until the onion is translucent and the potato and carrot are tender, stirring occasionally, about 15 minutes. Enjoy now or let cool to room temperature and refrigerate or freeze for later!

Indian Cheese Block *Paneer*

Paneer is an easy-to-make Indian homemade cheese that can be used to make many different dishes such as Cheese and Bell Pepper Skewers (page 108), Creamed Swiss Chard with Cheese Cubes (page 107), and Indian Cheese and Pea Curry (page 106). Once you make *paneer* you will be amazed at how easy it is to make cheese at home! To get the optimum yield and creamy taste and texture, it is best to use whole milk instead of reduced fat milk when making this cheese block. As a substitute you may use a firm tofu block and crumble it.

Makes ¼ lb (125 g)
Prep work: 5 minutes
Cook time: 5 minutes + 30 minutes sitting + 1 hour to set in the refrigerator
Refrigerator life: 1 day
Reheating method: None! Simply use to make desired dish.

4 cups (1 liter) whole milk
Juice of 1 lime

1 Pour the milk into a heavy bottomed, medium-sized stockpot. Slowly bring to a rolling boil over medium-high heat, stirring frequently as it comes to a boil. Don't let the milk boil over and out of the pot! Immediately turn off the heat.

2 Add the lime juice and gently stir for about 45 seconds, or until the milk separates into curds (solid cheese clumps) and whey (watery liquid). (If the milk does not separate, add more lime juice—2 teaspoons at a time—until it does.) The whey may appear to be light green in color from the lime juice. Turn off the heat.

3 Fold a large piece of cheesecloth into 4 layers (this will keep the cheese from falling through). Line a colander with the folded cheesecloth and place it over a large bowl to catch the whey. Gently pour the separated milk into the cheesecloth-lined colander. Let the whey drain through the colander down into the bowl.

4 When the whey has stopped draining (about 1 minute), gather up the sides of the cheesecloth to create a bundle. Using the back of a spoon, press the bundle against the side of the colander to squeeze out the excess whey. Be careful, as it will be hot.

5 Place the bundle on a plate. Unfold the cheesecloth and, using your hands (make sure it is not too hot to handle), mold the cheese into a square block about ¾ inch (2 cm) thick and neatly fold the cheesecloth back over it.

6 Pour the collected whey into the same pot that you boiled the milk in. Place the pot with the whey over the wrapped cheese block for 30 minutes to press any excess whey out of the cheese and allow it to firm up.

7 Remove the pot and discard the whey. Unfold the cheesecloth and gently place the cheese block on a clean plate. Cover with plastic wrap and refrigerate for a minimum of 1 hour and maximum of 1 day before cutting into cubes and/or pan-frying to make your favorite *paneer*-based dish!

How to Make the Indian Cheese Block

FIRST Curdled milk separated into curds (solid cheese clumps) and whey (watery liquid) after adding the lime juice to the boiling milk **SECOND** Pouring the curdled milk into a cheesecloth lined colander to collect the curds and drain the whey into a bowl.

THIRD Using the back of a spoon to squeeze out the excess whey from the bundle of cheese. **FOURTH** Cheese hand-molded into a square block

FIFTH Cheesecloth neatly folded over the square block of cheese. **SIXTH** Heavy pot with collected whey placed over the wrapped cheese block to press out excess whey and allow it to firm up.

SEVENTH Pressed cheese. **EIGHTH** Cover the cheese block with plastic wrap and refrigerate to further firm up before cutting into cubes

Indian Cheese and Pea Curry

A childhood favorite dish of mine, this is made with a firm style of Indian cheese that is cut into cubes, lightly pan-fried, and then simmered with peas in a savory curry. You may serve this dish with the Indian bread or with Plain Basmati Rice (page 63) or Rice with Cumin and Peas (page 64). When serving this dish, keep an eye out to make sure everyone gets an equal amount of cheese cubes, instead of being taken all by one person! Firm tofu may be substituted for the cheese.

Serves 3 to 4
Prep time: 10 minutes + 2 hours to make Indian Cheese Block, cubed and pan-fried (Using tofu will require less time)
Cook time: 25 minutes
Refrigerator life: 3 days
Freezer life: 1 month
Reheating method: Place the refrigerated or defrosted curry in a microwave, cover and stir periodically. Or, place it in a saucepan over medium-low heat and stir periodically.

Substitute tofu to make: Tofu and Peas Curry

3 tablespoons vegetable oil
1½ teaspoons peeled and finely grated fresh ginger
½ small onion, shredded on the largest grating holes of a box grater
1 fully ripe tomato, cut into 4 pieces
½ teaspoon ground turmeric
¼ teaspoon ground red pepper (cayenne)
½ teaspoon salt
½ teaspoon ground black pepper
½ cup (60 g) frozen or fresh green peas
1 recipe Indian Cheese Block (page 110) or ½ block firm tofu (about ½ lb/225 g), cubed and pan-fried
1¼ cups (300 ml) water

1 Pour the oil into a medium saucepan and place over medium heat. When the oil is heated, add the ginger and onion. Sauté until the onion is golden brown, stirring frequently, about 5 minutes.
2 Reduce the heat to medium-low. Add the tomato and cover the saucepan. Cook until the tomato becomes completely soft and mashed and is combined with the onion to form a coarse paste, stirring every minute or so and lightly mashing the tomato, about 5 minutes.

3 Add the turmeric, red pepper, salt, and black pepper. Stir to combine. Cook uncovered for 6 minutes, stirring frequently.
4 Add the peas, pan-fried cheese cubes (or tofu), and water. Stir to combine.

Bring to a rolling boil over high heat.
5 Stir and reduce the heat to medium. Simmer uncovered for 5 minutes, stirring occasionally. Enjoy now or let cool to room temperature and refrigerate or freeze for later!

Creamed Swiss Chard with Cheese Cubes

Chard, commonly called Swiss chard, are leafy greens with beautiful long stalks. My recipe for chard is inspired from the Indian creamed spinach and cheese cubes dish, *saag paneer*, or more accurately *palak paneer*, to which I added chard. This dish goes best with Baked Whole Wheat Flatbreads (page 54), or may be served with Plain Basmati Rice (page 63) or Rice with Cumin and Peas (page 64). Look for chard that is not wilted, with stalks that are firm and crisp. I keep it in the refrigerator for up to 3 days. Firm tofu and coconut milk may be substituted for the cheese and heavy cream to make this a vegan dish.

Serves 3 to 4

Prep time: 10 minutes + 1 hour, 50 minutes to make Indian Cheese Block, cubed and pan-fried (using tofu will require less time)

Cook time: 40 minutes

Refrigerator life: 3 days

Freezer life: 1 month

Reheating method: Place the refrigerated or defrosted chard and cheese (or tofu) in a microwave, cover and stir periodically. Or, place it in a saucepan over medium-low heat and stir periodically.

Substitute tofu to make: Creamed Swiss Chard with Tofu

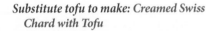

- **1 lb (500 g) fresh Swiss chard (rainbow, ruby red, or rhubarb) (1 bunch)**
- **½ lb (225 g) fresh spinach (1 bunch) or baby spinach**
- **1 fully ripe tomato, cut into 4 pieces**
- **¼ teaspoon ground red pepper (cayenne)**
- **½ teaspoon salt**
- **½ teaspoon ground black pepper**
- **2 tablespoons vegetable oil**
- **1½ teaspoons peeled and finely grated fresh ginger**
- **½ small onion, finely diced**
- **1 fresh finger-length green chili pepper, finely diced (any variety)**
- **1 recipe Indian Cheese Block (page 104) or ½ block firm tofu (about ½ lb/225 g), cubed and pan-fried (page 110)**
- **½ cup (125 ml) heavy cream or coconut milk**

1 Thoroughly wash the chard. Trim the bottom ¼ inch (6 mm) off the stems and discard. Stack a few stalks of chard together and cut them, starting from the stem end, crosswise into ¼-inch (6 mm) pieces. When you get to the leafy part, bunch the leaves together and keep cutting into ¼-inch (6 mm) pieces.

2 Trim the bottom 1 inch (2.5 cm) off the stems of the spinach bunch and discard. Thoroughly wash the spinach. Coarsely chop the leaves and remaining stems. If using baby spinach, you do not need to trim the stems or chop the leaves.

3 Squeeze the chopped greens and stems with your hands to remove any excess water and place them in a large saucepan over medium heat. Add the tomato and cook for 10 minutes. You will soon see some water released from the greens as they start to reduce in volume.

4 Add the red pepper, salt, and black pepper. Stir to combine and cover. Cook for 10 minutes so the greens become tender, stirring occasionally.

5 Remove the cover and cook until most or all of the water has cooked off, stirring occasionally, about 10 minutes. The greens will be moist and mushy. Turn off the heat.

6 Transfer the cooked greens and stems to a blender. Purée until smooth, but do not liquefy it, and then put the puréed contents back into the saucepan.

7 Pour the oil into a small skillet and place over medium heat. When the oil is heated, add the ginger, onion, and green chili pepper. Sauté until the onion is browned, stirring frequently, about 5 minutes. Pour into the saucepan with the blended greens.

8 Add the cheese cubes (or tofu) and heavy cream (or coconut milk). Stir to combine. Simmer for 5 minutes over medium heat, stirring occasionally. Enjoy now or let cool to room temperature and refrigerate or freeze for later!

Cheese and Bell Pepper Skewers

These delicious kebabs are a colorful Indian appetizer made from bell peppers and Indian cheese cubes that is often served at Indian wedding receptions, but you certainly do not have to wait for a wedding to enjoy them! When entertaining, I like to place the cheese cubes and bell peppers on decorative mini skewers with a pretty ribbon on the end. Fresh Coriander Chutney (page 37) can also be offered for light dipping. Just be sure to make plenty of kebabs, because they tend to get eaten up quickly! Tofu may be substituted for the cheese as well.

Serves 3 to 4
Prep time: 10 minutes + 2 hours to make Indian Cheese Block (tofu will take less time)
Cook time: 25 minutes resting
Refrigerator Life: 2 days
Reheating Method: Place the refrigerated cheese and bell peppers in a warmed oven (about 350°F/175°C) and heat. A less preferred method is to heat the cheese and bell peppers in a microwave.

Substitute tofu to make: Sautéed Tofu and Bell Pepper Skewers

1 recipe Indian Cheese Block (page 104) or ½ block firm tofu (about ½ lb/125 g) (see note)
3 tablespoons vegetable oil
½ small onion, shredded on the largest grating holes of a box grater
1 fully ripe tomato, coarsely chopped
½ teaspoon cumin seeds
¼ teaspoon ground red pepper (cayenne)
¾ teaspoon salt
½ teaspoon ground black pepper
½ green bell pepper, cut into 8 pieces
½ red bell pepper, cut into 8 pieces
8 to 16 mini bamboo skewers (about 4 to 6 inches/10 to 15 cm)

1 Cut the Indian Cheese Block into 16 even cubes. It is okay if the pieces are not perfectly square cubes.
2 Pour the oil into a medium nonstick skillet and place over medium heat. When the oil is heated, add the onion. Sauté until the onion is golden brown, stirring frequently, about 5 minutes.
3 Reduce the heat to medium-low. Add the tomato and cover the skillet. Cook until the tomato becomes completely soft and mashed and is combined with the onion to form a coarse paste, stirring every minute

or so and lightly mashing the tomato, about 5 minutes.
4 Add the cumin seeds, red pepper, ½ teaspoon of the salt and ¼ teaspoon of the black pepper. Stir to combine. Cook uncovered for 2 minutes, stirring frequently. This is the *masala* (spice base).
5 Increase the heat to medium. Add the cheese cubes (or tofu). Gently mix to combine. Cook uncovered for 2 minutes, gently stirring frequently and turning the cheese cubes. Push the cheese cubes and *masala* to one side of the skillet.
6 Add the red and green bell peppers to the other side of the skillet. Sprinkle the remaining ¼ teaspoon of the salt, and ¼ teaspoon of the black pepper on the bell peppers. Cook uncovered until the bell peppers are just tender with some slight crispness, stirring occasionally, about 5 minutes. While the bell peppers are cooking, gently turn the cheese cubes occasionally so they do not burn.
7 Turn off the heat and cover the skillet. Let rest on the warm stovetop for 5 minutes.
8 On each skewer, thread alternate pieces of the green bell pepper, cheese cube, and red bell pepper, depending on the length of the toothpick. Enjoy now or let cool to room temperature and refrigerate for later.

TOFU DIRECTIONS:
1 Place the half tofu block between two folded kitchen towels on a cutting board. Place a heavy weight (such as a heavy bottomed pot one-fourth filled with water) on top of the tofu block for 20 minutes to press any excess water out of the tofu.
2 Remove the weight from the tofu block. Cut the tofu block into 16 even pieces. Continue with steps 2 to 8 above, replacing the cheese with tofu. In step 5, let cook for 5 minutes.

Garam Masala
Roasted Spice Mix

This roasted spice mix is made by dry roasting a specific blend of whole spices and then grinding them into a fine powder. Spending a few minutes making this spice mix at home instead of buying it will ensure you have fresh, aromatic spices to add to your dishes.

Makes ½ cup (40 g)
Cook time: 5 minutes
Shelf life: Store up to 3 months in an airtight container at room temperature.

½ cup (30 g) coriander seeds
½ teaspoon whole cloves
6 whole green cardamoms
1 tablespoon cumin seeds
¼ teaspoon black peppercorns
One 1 inch (2.5 cm) cinnamon stick

1 Place a small skillet over medium heat. When the skillet is heated, roast the coriander seeds until they are lightly brown and fragrant, stirring frequently, about 2 minutes. Remove from the skillet and set aside.
2 Roast the remaining spices in the same skillet over medium heat until they are fragrant, stirring frequently, about 1 minute. Do not let the cumin seeds burn and turn black. Immediately remove the spices from the skillet and place in a small bowl. Let cool slightly before grinding.
3 Place about half of the roasted seeds and spices in a coffee/spice grinder and grind to a fine powder. Place the ground spices in a small bowl. Repeat with the second half of the roasted seeds and spices.
4 Use now or place in an airtight container at room temperature up to 3 months.

Pan-Fried Cheese Cubes

Refrigerate a block of homemade Indian cheese (*paneer*) for at least an hour to cut into cubes and pan-fry. Traditionally, the cubes are deep-fried before putting them in the main dishes, but I lightly pan-fry the cubes, which is a bit easier and healthier! For best results, it is essential to use a non-stick skillet when pan-frying the cheese cubes so they will not break apart.

Makes about 16 cubes
Prep work: 5 minutes
Cook time: 5 minutes
Refrigerator life: 3 days
Freezer life: 1 month
Reheating method: None. Simply drop the refrigerated or frozen pan-fried cheese cubes into the dish you are making.

Substitute tofu to make: Pan-Fried Tofu Cubes

1 recipe Indian Cheese Block (page 104) or ½ block firm tofu (about ½ lb/125 g) (see note below and steps on page 111)
3 tablespoons vegetable oil

1 Prepare Indian Cheese Block (page 105) or, if using tofu cubes, use the method described on page 111.
2 Cut the Indian Cheese Block into 16 even cubes. It is okay if the pieces are not perfectly square cubes.
3 Pour the oil into a medium nonstick skillet and place over medium heat. When the oil is heated, add the cheese cubes. Pan-fry the cheese cubes until all the sides, or at least the top and bottom sides are lightly golden, gently turning frequently, about 3 minutes.
4 Remove the cubes from the skillet and place on paper towels to drain excess oil.
5 The fried cheese cubes may be used in a recipe now or they may be placed in an airtight container and refrigerated or frozen for later use.

> **NOTE:** Firm tofu usually comes in 14 to 16 ounce (400 g to 500 g) blocks. Since we are using half a block of tofu in this recipe, you may store the unused portion submerged in cold water in a covered bowl in the refrigerator for up to 2 days.

How to Compress the Tofu Block

FIRST Place the half tofu block between two folded kitchen towels on a cutting board.

SECOND Place a heavy weight on top of the tofu block for 20 minutes to press any excess water out of the tofu.

THIRD Remove the weight from the tofu block. Cut the tofu block into 16 even pieces. Continue with steps 3 to 5 in the recipe on page 110. In step 3, let it cook for 10 minutes while turning the tofu pieces frequently. Keep a cover on the skillet to prevent oil splatters from the tofu's moisture.

Tofu Breakfast Scramble

This scrambled tofu breakfast dish is inspired by my mom's Indian-style scrambled eggs recipe. The tofu remains moist like real eggs since I don't press the water out before cooking as I do with other tofu dishes. I tricked my dad when I made this dish the first time since he thought it was made from real eggs! The scrambled tofu can be placed between two slices of toast for a tofu scramble sandwich. You can also make a Mexican-style breakfast burrito by placing the scrambled tofu in a warm white flour tortilla, sprinkling on your favorite cheese, adding some salsa, and rolling it all up!

Serves 2 to 3
Prep time: 5 minutes
Cook time: 20 minutes
Refrigerator life: 2 days
Reheating method: Place the refrigerated tofu dish in a skillet over medium-low heat and stir periodically. Or, place the tofu dish in a microwave and stir periodically.

3 tablespoons vegetable oil
1 small onion, diced
1 small fully ripe tomato, such as plum (Roma), diced
1 fresh finger-length green chili pepper, sliced into thin circles (any variety)
¼ teaspoon ground turmeric
¼ teaspoon ground red pepper (cayenne)
½ teaspoon salt
½ teaspoon ground black pepper
½ block firm tofu (about ½ lb/125 g) (see note)
1 small handful fresh coriander leaves (cilantro), rinsed and chopped

1 Pour the oil into a medium nonstick skillet and place over medium heat.

When the oil is heated, add the onion. Sauté until the onion is translucent, stirring frequently, about 3 minutes.

2 Add the tomato. Cook until the tomato pieces become soft, stirring frequently, about 5 minutes. Add the green chili pepper, turmeric, red pepper, salt, and black pepper. Stir to combine.

3 Hold the tofu block over the skillet and crumble it apart with your fingers. Cook for 10 minutes, while further breaking apart the tofu into small pieces and stirring frequently. Turn off the heat. Enjoy now or let cool to room temperature and refrigerate for later! Just before serving, stir in the chopped coriander leaves.

> **NOTE:** Firm tofu usually comes in 14 to 16 ounce (400 g to 500 g) blocks. Since we are using half a block of tofu in this recipe, store the unused portion submerged in cold water in a covered bowl and refrigerate for up to 2 days. Unlike other tofu recipes, I do not press the water out of the tofu here so that I may get a consistency closer to eggs.

Indian Cheese with Peas

After making homemade crumbled Indian cheese, it only takes minutes to cook it with some tomatoes, onion, peas, and spices to create a delicious dish. This dish can be served with the Baked Whole Wheat Flatbreads (page 54). The only problem with this dish is that I can easily eat too much of it since it is one of my favorite *paneer* (Indian cheese) dishes! Firm tofu may be substituted for the cheese.

TOFU DIRECTIONS:

1 If using tofu, place the tofu block between two folded kitchen towels on a cutting board. Place a heavy weight on top of the tofu block for 20 minutes to press any excess water out of the tofu.

2 Remove the weight from the tofu block. Pour the oil into a medium nonstick skillet and place over medium heat. When the oil is heated, add the onion. Sauté until the onion is golden brown, stirring frequently, about 5 minutes.

3 Reduce the heat to medium-low. Add the tomato. Cover the skillet. Cook until the tomato becomes completely soft and mashed and is combined with the onion to form a coarse paste, stirring every minute or so and lightly mashing the tomato, about 5 minutes, stirring frequently.

4 Hold the tofu block over the saucepan and crumble it apart with your fingers. Add the turmeric, red pepper, and salt. Increase the heat to medium. Stir to combine and cook for 5 minutes.

5 Add the peas and stir to combine. Cook for another 5 minutes, stirring frequently. Enjoy now or let cool to room temperature and refrigerate for later!

Serves 2 to 3
Prep time: 5 minutes + 10 minutes to make the Crumbled Indian Cheese
Cook time: 20 minutes
Refrigerator life: 2 days
Reheating method: Place the refrigerated dish in a skillet over medium-low heat and stir periodically. Or, place the dish in a microwave and stir periodically.

Substitute tofu to make: Crumbled Tofu with Peas

1 recipe **Crumbled Indian Cheese (page106) or ½ block firm tofu (about ½ lb/125 g) (see note below)**
3 tablespoons **vegetable oil**
½ small **onion, shredded on the largest grating hole of a box grater**
1 small fully ripe **tomato, such as plum (Roma), diced**
½ cup (60 g) frozen or fresh **green peas**
½ teaspoon **turmeric**
½ teaspoon **ground red pepper (cayenne)**
½ teaspoon **salt**

1 Pour the oil into a medium nonstick skillet and place over medium heat. When the oil is heated, add the onion. Sauté until the onion is golden brown, stirring frequently, about 5 minutes.

2 Reduce the heat to medium-low. Add the tomato. Cover the skillet. Cook until the tomato is soft and mashed and is combined with the onion to form a coarse paste, stir every minute or so while lightly mashing the tomato, about 5 minutes.

3 Add the cheese, peas, turmeric, red pepper, and salt. Stir to combine. Increase the heat to medium. Cook until the cheese slightly darkens in color to a golden-yellow shade, stirring frequently and breaking apart the cheese into small pieces, about 7 minutes.

4 Enjoy now or let cool to room temperature and refrigerate for later.

NOTE: Firm tofu usually comes in 14 to 16 ounce (400 g to 500 g) blocks. Since we are using half a block of tofu here, you may store the unused portion submerged in cold water in a covered bowl and refrigerate for up to 2 days.

Tandoori Tofu Kebabs

As the name suggests, a "tandoori" item is traditionally cooked in a *tandoor*, which is an open fit pit heated with coal or wood. You can get similar results in a traditional home oven, toaster oven, or you may even use an outdoor grill. Here I show you how to make *tandoori* tofu easily in your toaster oven. Because tofu has so much natural moisture, it will not easily dry out. This means you can make this dish ahead of time and then place the cooked tofu in a serving platter, cover it with foil, and keep it in the warm oven until dinner is served. Tandoori Tofu Kebabs goes well with Plain Basmati Rice (page 63) or Rice with Cumin and Peas (page 64). You can also serve them with Fresh Coriander Chutney (page 37).

Serves 3 to 4
Prep time: 15 minutes + 20 minutes sitting + 1 hour marinating
Cook time: 30 minutes
Refrigerator Life: 2 days
Reheating Method: Place the refrigerated tofu kebabs in a warmed oven (about 350°F/175°C) and heat. A less preferred method is to heat the tofu kebabs in a microwave.

1 block firm tofu (about 1 lb/500 g) (see note below)
1 tablespoon vegetable oil
Four to six 12 in (30.5 cm) wooden skewers
1 small red onion, cut into 8 wedges and layers separated
Juice of 1 lime

MARINADE
1 tablespoon minced garlic
Juice of 1 lime
3 tablespoons vegetable oil
¾ teaspoon cumin seeds, roasted and ground (see page 20)
½ teaspoon ground coriander
1 teaspoon paprika
½ teaspoon ground red pepper (cayenne)
¾ teaspoon salt
½ teaspoon ground black pepper
1½ teaspoons plain yogurt or plain soy yogurt

1 Place the tofu block between two folded kitchen towels on a cutting board. Place a heavy weight (such as a heavy bottomed pot one-fourth filled with water) on top of the tofu block for 20 minutes to press any excess water out of the tofu.
2 Remove the weight from the tofu block. Cut the tofu block into 32 even pieces. Spread out the cut pieces in a dish or plate.
3 Place all of the ingredients for the Marinade in a small bowl. Mix well. Pour half of the Marinade evenly over the tofu pieces. You may use a spoon or your fingers to spread it out. Turn over the tofu pieces and pour the rest of the Marinade over them, making sure all sides of the tofu pieces are coated with Marinade.

Cover the dish and let rest at room temperature for 1 hour or refrigerate for up to 1 day. At this time, place the wooden skewers in a shallow dish with water to soak them for 30 minutes so they do not burn when in the oven.
4 Preheat the oven to 400°F (200°C). While the oven is heating up, spread 1 tablespoon of the oil evenly on a baking sheet. Thread alternate pieces of tofu and onion slices on the wooden skewers. Lay the skewers on the oiled baking sheet.
5 When the oven is heated, bake the skewers for 15 minutes. Turn the skewers and bake 15 minutes more.
6 Remove the skewers from the oven. Sprinkle the lime juice evenly on the skewers. Enjoy now or let cool to room temperature and refrigerate for later!

NOTE: Firm tofu usually comes in 14-to 16-ounce (400 g to 500 g) blocks, so as long as it is around this weight (about 1 lb/500 g), it is okay.

CHAPTER 7

A Fruitful Ending: Drinks & Desserts

Sugar and spice make everything nice, and when you add fresh fruits and vegetables it makes drinks and desserts a tad bit healthy too.

A fun and refreshing way to enjoy fruits and vegetables is to blend them up or juice them. Refreshing yogurt-based fruit smoothies, known as lassi in India, made with strawberries or sweet peaches are one of my daughter's favorite drinks. If you prefer lighter fruit drinks, you will enjoy my mixed fruit juice made with juicy oranges, grapefruit, and tropical pineapple. Vegetables such as spinach, carrots, and tomatoes also combine together for a highly beneficial and delicious juice. And to just have a little moment of bliss, sip my Chai Tea (page 119) or Indian Cappuccino (page 118).

For an exotic summer ice cream treat, try my Mango Ice Cream (page 121) with a hint of cardamom. Fresh berries and other fruits mixed into eggless vanilla custard is an elegant way to enjoy fruits. Melons such as watermelon, honey dew melon, and cantaloupe are royally divine when dipped into a sweet syrup infused with rose water. Carrots make a rich dessert when cooked with milk, sweetened with sugar, and then sprinkled with crushed cardamom seeds and slivered almonds. My favorite dessert in this chapter is the Chocolate and Coconut Covered Cherries (page 124), since I absolutely love chocolate and it goes great with coconut and fresh cherries, making this a yummy, beautiful dessert that is fun to eat!

So occasionally go ahead and have seconds for drinks and dessert because fruits and veggies are good for you!

Strawberry Lassi

Sweet red strawberries make one of my daughter's favorite lassi drinks (even though I leave out the sugar when I make it for her!). A lassi is an Indian smoothie, which is a refreshing drink made from fruit and yogurt, with mango lassi being the most popular. It can be served for breakfast, as a cocktail, a dessert, or anytime you wish. I keep my strawberries for up to five days in the refrigerator; after that they tend to shrivel or mold. Strawberries have lots of vitamin C, which is an effective antioxidant that can help prevent cancer and helps heal cuts and wounds.

Serves 2
Prep time: 5 minutes
Refrigerator life: 2 days, shake before using

½ lb (225 g) strawberries (about 15 strawberries)
4 tablespoons plain yogurt or plain soy yogurt (regular or fat free)
4 tablespoons sugar (you can use less sugar if the strawberries are very sweet)
¼ cup (65 ml) water
5 ice cubes plus crushed ice to half fill 2 tall glasses

1 Wash the strawberries. Cut off the leafy stems and discard.
2 Place the strawberries, yogurt, sugar, water, and 5 ice cubes in a blender. Blend until smooth and the ice is crushed. If you are making this drink for later, store in the refrigerator now and shake vigorously before serving.
3 Fill 2 tall glasses half-way with the crushed ice. Pour the lassi into the glasses and enjoy with a straw!

Variation
Peach Lassi

Nothing beats biting into a sweet, ripe and juicy fresh peach, but I think my peach lassi on a hot summer day totally beats the heat! Look for peaches that are slightly soft to the touch and have a fragrant aroma. If I only find firm peaches, I keep them in my fruit bowl at room temperature until they soften, and then I refrigerate them for up to five days. Peaches are good for healthy eyesight, cancer prevention, and lung health.

1 Wash 2 peaches. Using a small knife, cut each peach in half lengthwise around the pit. Hold a peach in both hands and twist the halves in opposite directions to separate them. Pry the pit out with a knife discard. Coarsely chop up the peach halves with their skin on. Repeat with the other peach.
2 Place the chopped peaches, ½ cup (125 g) plain yogurt or plain soy yogurt, ½ cup (100 g) sugar, ¼ cup (65 ml) water and 15 ice cubes in a blender. You can use less sugar if the peaches are very sweet. Blend until smooth and the ice is crushed. If you are making this drink for later, store in the refrigerator now and shake before serving.
3 Fill 2 tall glasses half-way with the crushed ice. Pour the lassi into the glasses and enjoy with a straw!

Fresh Fruit Juice

Peach Lassi

Fresh Vegetable Juice

Strawberry Lassi

Fresh Vegetable Juice

Different combinations of vegetables can be juiced to create healthy juices. When my mom was in her teens, she used to make this spinach, tomato, and carrot juice for her older sister (as per doctor's orders for healthy eyes) in return for help on her physics homework. My mom only had a hand juicer instead of today's electric juicers, so it was quite an effort, but she did it so her sister's eyes would get better (and her physics grades got better as well!).

Serves 2
Prep time: 10 minutes
Refrigerator life: 1 day, shake before serving

½ lb (225 g) fresh spinach (about 1 bunch) or baby spinach
2 ripe tomatoes
2 medium carrots, peeled and cut into thick matchsticks (see page 23)
½ teaspoon salt
½ teaspoon ground black pepper

1 Trim the bottom 1 inch (2.5 cm) off the stems of the spinach bunch and discard. Thoroughly wash the spinach. Coarsely chop the leaves and remaining stems. If using baby spinach, you do not need to trim the stems or chop the leaves.
2 Wash the tomatoes and coarsely chop them.
3 Wash the carrots. Coarsely chop them.
4 Juice the spinach, tomatoes, and carrots through a juicer.
5 Add the salt and black pepper. Mix well. There may be froth on the surface of the juice, which is okay. Enjoy now or chill briefly in the refrigerator.

Fresh Fruit Juice

When on vacation in India or Mexico, the juice carts of street vendors always entices me. I especially enjoy freshly squeezed sweet pineapples and oranges combined with a bit of tartness from a grapefruit. Sweet, ripe pineapples are brown instead of green on the outside. I use my electric juicer to make this juice to enjoy a taste of the tropics anytime!

Serves 2 to 3
Prep time: 10 minutes
Refrigerator life: 1 day, shake before serving

½ pineapple
3 oranges
1 grapefruit
½ teaspoon salt
¼ teaspoon ground black pepper

1 If you have a whole pineapple, slice of the top and discard. Cut the pineapple crosswise in half. Cut one half of the pineapple crosswise in half again to get two pineapple rounds. Lay one round flat and cut around the inside of the rind. Remove the rind and discard. Cut out the inside core and discard. Chop up the pineapple rounds into 1-inch (2.5 cm) pieces. Wrap the other half of the pineapple in plastic wrap and refrigerate for up to 2 days to enjoy later.
2 Cut off the top and bottom of the oranges and grapefruit. Using a small knife, score the oranges and grapefruit from the top to bottom, cutting only skin-deep, into four or five sections. Use your fingers to peel away the skin and discard. Pry apart the orange and grapefruit slices.
3 Juice the pineapple, oranges, and grapefruit through a juicer.
4 Add the salt and black pepper. Mix well. There may be froth on the surface of the juice, which is okay. Enjoy now or chill briefly in the refrigerator.

Indian Cappuccino

This cappuccino is my mom's signature drink she offers at the end of her dinner parties, and it is always a hit. It has a delicious creamy froth that is easy to get without using fancy milk-frothing machines. Simply pour the milk into the glass from as high a distance as you can, and watch the froth form! Making the cappuccino batter does require a bit of patience and a lot of arm strength to get it perfect and fluffy, but it can be made in advance and refrigerated. The batter actually comes out fluffier and more ideal when making it for four cups of cappuccino, and the rest can be saved for later. In addition to getting the energy boost we may need sometimes from the caffeine in coffee, studies are now showing caffeine is linked to lower depression risk in women.

Serves 2
Prep time: 11 minutes (Cappuccino Batter can be made 3 days in advance and refrigerated)
Cook time: 5 minutes

Chai Tea

Indian Cappuccino

1 cup (250 ml) whole milk (see note)
½ cup (125 ml) water

For garnish: 2 pinches of either coffee granules, cocoa
    powder, ground cinnamon or ground nutmeg

CAPPUCCINO BATTER (MAKES BATTER FOR 4 CUPS)
4 teaspoons instant coffee granules
8 teaspoons sugar
4 teaspoons water

1 To make the Cappuccino Batter: Thoroughly mix
together the coffee granules, sugar, and 1 teaspoon of the
water in a small bowl for 2 minutes.
2 Add another 1 teaspoon of the water. Beat vigorously
for 3 minutes with a spoon. The color will become light
brown and the mixture will start to become creamy. It is
important to add the water a little bit at time, and then
beat vigorously so the water is absorbed and air is beaten
in, allowing the batter to become light and fluffy, which
leads to more froth when making the cappuccino.
3 Add another 1 teaspoon of the water. Beat vigorously
for 3 minutes with a spoon.
4 Add the remaining 1 teaspoon of the water. Beat
vigorously for 3 minutes with a spoon. The mixture will
become light brown and creamy like a thick pudding.
Divide the batter in half to use for now and cover and
refrigerate the other half for up to 3 days.
5 To make Indian Cappuccino, evenly divide half of the
batter into 2 parts and put into each of the 2 cups.
6 Pour the milk and water into a small saucepan. Bring
to a rolling boil over high heat, stirring occasionally as
it comes to a boil. Don't let the milk boil over and out of
the saucepan! Immediately turn off the heat.
7 Put 2 tablespoons of the boiled milk in each cup. Stir
to mix the batter and the milk. Pour the remainder of
the boiled milk evenly into each cup from at least 6
inches (15 cm) above the cup to allow the froth to form.
Sprinkle a pinch of coffee granules, cocoa, cinnamon, or
nutmeg on top of the froth for garnish. Enjoy!

> **NOTE:** If using reduced fat milk or fat free milk, use
> 1½ cups (375 ml) of milk and no water.
>   If using a vegan or soy milk you will get a different
> taste than you get with traditional dairy.

Chai Tea

After tea became increasingly popular in
Europe, the British established tea cultivation in India in the 1800s to satisfy the new
European thirst. Since then, tea cultivation
has flourished in India, and India is one of
the top producers of tea. Indian tea is enjoyed
in coffee shops worldwide. I see it commonly
called "chai tea" but because the word chai
means tea it literally tranlates to "tea tea."
Tea may also be infused with spices such as
ginger, cloves, and cardamoms to make a masala
chai. I use cardamoms in this recipe, which help
in digestion and soothes your stomach.

Serves 2
Cook time: 5 minutes

1½ cups (375 ml) water
2 bags black tea or 1 tablespoon loose black tea
2 whole green cardamom pods
½ cup (125 ml) whole milk (see note below)
4 teaspoons sugar

1 Place the water and bagged or loose tea in a small
saucepan. Open the cardamom pods (see page 20 for how
to open them) and add the seeds and the pods. Bring to a
rolling boil over high heat.
2 Add the milk and bring to a rolling boil again. Don't let
the milk boil over and out of the saucepan! Immediately
reduce the heat to medium.
3 Simmer the tea for 2½ minutes, stirring occasionally.
4 Pour the tea through a small sieve evenly into 2 cups.
Discard the cardamom seeds and pods, and the tea bags
or loose tea collected in the sieve.
5 Add 2 teaspoons of sugar to each cup, stir and enjoy!

> **NOTE:** If you're using reduced fat milk, use 1 cup (250 ml)
> of water and 1 cup (250 ml) of milk.
>   If you're using fat free milk, use ½ cup (125 ml) of water
> and 1½ cups (375 ml) of milk.
>   If using a vegan or soy milk you will get a different taste
> than you get with traditional dairy.

Melon Balls in Rose Syrup

To make this fun, delectable dessert, I use a simple kitchen tool called a melon baller and scoop out colorful little spheres of fresh melon varieties. Then I chill the balled fruit in a sugar syrup infused with rose water. This dish will surely impress your guests visually and with its divine taste. Melons are low in calories and a good source of potassium and vitamin C, which help fight off diseases in our body. I usually ball extra melons and pack them in my daughter's lunchbox so she can enjoy fresh fruit in a fun round shape.

Serves 7
Prep time: 10 minutes
Cook time: 15 minutes + 25 minutes cooling + 2 hours to chill
Refrigerator life: 1 day
Reheating Method: None. Serve chilled.

1 cup (200 g) sugar
2 cups (500 ml) water
1 cantaloupe
1 honey dew melon
1 small seedless watermelon
2 tablespoons rose water

1 To make the syrup, bring the sugar and water to a rolling boil in a medium saucepan over high heat.
2 Reduce the heat to medium. Simmer for 15 minutes. Remove from the heat and let cool to room temperature.
3 To ball the cantaloupe, cut it in half crosswise. Using a spoon, scoop out any seeds and strings and discard. Using a melon baller, scoop out 9 balls. Cover the rest of the cantaloupe with plastic wrap and refrigerate for up to 3 days to enjoy later.
4 Ball the honey dew melon the same way as the cantaloupe and scoop out 9 balls. Cover the rest of the honey dew melon with plastic wrap and refrigerate for up to 3 days to enjoy later
5 To ball the watermelon, cut it in half crosswise. Using a melon baller, scoop out 10 balls. Cover the rest of the watermelon with plastic wrap and refrigerate for up to 3 days to enjoy later.
6 When the syrup has cooled to room temperature, add the rose water. Stir to combine. Add the cantaloupe, honeydew melon, and watermelon balls. Cover and place in the refrigerator until chilled, or up to one day. When serving, place 4 melon balls per person in a dessert bowl, and add plenty of the rose syrup. Enjoy!

> **NOTE:** A cantaloupe and a honeydew melon yield about 40 balls each. A small watermelon yields about 60 balls total. You may choose any combination of fruits to ball for your dessert.

Mango Ice Cream

Mangoes are the quintessential fruit of India. They come in many different varieties, shapes, colors and sizes, and are enjoyed in many different ways from chutneys, drinks, ice cream, and of course eaten as a fresh fruit. When buying ripe mangoes, look for mangoes that yield slightly to the touch and have a sweet fragrance. The skin will be yellow-orange or green and have red blushing, and the flesh will be bright yellow, and hopefully sweet and fragrant. When unripe, mangoes will have firm and mostly green skin. Place unripe mangoes in a paper bag at room temperature for a few days until they soften, and then refrigerate them for up to one week. Mangoes make a wonderful Indian ice cream. Indian ice cream is not churned during freezing resulting in a denser textured ice cream. Mangoes improve digestion and help with constipation. They are also high in iron and good for pregnant women and for people with anemia.

flesh in a blender. Blend until puréed smooth.

5 After the milk has cooled to room temperature, add the puréed mango to the milk. Stir thoroughly to combine. Pour the mixture into ice cream bar molds or an ice cube tray or mini muffin pan tray, or any shape mold you prefer. Put in the freezer until frozen, about 3 hours.

6 Remove the frozen ice cream from the molds by tilting the mold or tray sideways and running under hot water until the ice cream is loose and you can take it out. Enjoy!

Serves 4 to 6
Prep time: 10 minutes
Cook time: 25 minutes + 25 minutes cooling + 3 hours to set in the freezer
Freezer life: 3 weeks

2 cups (500 ml) whole milk or plain soy milk
Seeds from 5 whole green cardamom pods, crushed (see page 20)
½ cup (100 g) sugar
1 large fully ripe mango (about 1 lb/500 g)

1 Pour the milk into a heavy bottomed, medium-sized saucepan. Bring to a rolling boil over high heat, stirring frequently as it comes to a boil. Don't let the milk boil over and out of the saucepan! Immediately reduce the heat to medium.

2 Add the crushed cardamom seeds and stir to combine. Simmer the milk until it is reduced to ½ cup (125 ml), stirring frequently, about 20 to 25 minutes. If any skin forms on the surface, simply stir it back in. If there is any scorched milk at the bottom of the saucepan, do not scrape it.

3 Add the sugar and stir until it has all dissolved. Remove from heat and let cool to room temperature to avoid adding fresh mango to hot milk.

4 Wash the mango. Using a vegetable peeler, peel the mango. Cut away all of the flesh from the pit. Place the mango

Fruit Custard

A common Indian dessert, you can choose your favorite fresh fruits to put in this custard, keeping in mind that berries look pretty and taste great (plus, they are excellent sources of antioxidants).

Serves 2
Prep time: 3 hours to chill in the refrigerator
Cook time: 10 minutes
Refrigerator life: up to 1 day before adding the fruit

2 cups (500 ml) plus 1 tablespoon plus 1 teaspoon whole milk
1 tablespoon plus 1 teaspoon cornstarch
2 tablespoons sugar
½ teaspoon vanilla extract
5 green grapes, sliced in half lengthwise
½ banana
2 strawberries, diced into ¼-inch (6-mm) pieces

1 Pour 2 cups (500 ml) of the milk into a heavy bottomed, medium-sized sauce-pan. Bring to a rolling boil over high heat, stirring frequently as it comes to a boil. Don't let the milk boil over and out of the saucepan! Immediately reduce the heat to medium.

2 Simmer the milk until it is reduced to 1¼ cups (300 ml), stirring frequently, about 10 minutes. If any skin forms on the surface, simply stir it back in. If there is any scorched milk at the bottom of the saucepan, do not scrape it.

3 Put the remaining 1 tablespoon plus 1 teaspoon of milk in a small bowl. Add the cornstarch. Using a small spoon, quickly mix together until thoroughly combined and smooth without any lumps. Add this mixture to the saucepan, stirring continuously for 1 minute to ensure lumps do not form in the milk.

4 Add the sugar and stir until it has all dissolved. Turn off the heat. Add the va-nilla extract and stir to combine. Transfer to a bowl to let cool to room temperature so it will thicken. Cover and refrigerate to chill to the consistency of custard, about 3 hours. The custard will thicken more.

5 Remove the chilled custard from the refrigerator and mix. Cut the banana half into 4 equal lengthwise segments. Cut each segment crosswise into ¼-inch (6 mm) pieces.

6 Add the banana, grapes and strawberry to the chilled custard and mix well.

> **NOTE:** You may also make Berry Custard with blueberries, black berries, strawberries, and raspberries. Whatever combination of berries you use, I would suggest to also adding a banana since it gives the custard a nice sweet taste.

Sweetened Carrots

Serves 4
Prep time: 10 minutes
Cook time: 45-55 minutes
Refrigerator Life: 5 days
Freezer Life: 1 month
Reheating Method: This dessert might harden a bit in the refrigerator, but will soften when heated. To heat, place the refrigerated or defrosted sweetened carrots in a microwave and stir periodically. Or, place it in a saucepan over medium-low heat and stir periodically.

2 medium carrots, peeled
4 cups (1 liter) whole milk or plain soy milk
¼ cup (65 ml) half-and-half
1 tablespoon blanched, slivered almonds (see page 21)
½ cup (100 g) sugar
Seeds from 2 cardamom pods, crushed (see page 20)

Shredded carrots cooked in sweetened milk combine into a rich and creamy Indian dessert called *gajar ka halwa*. This dish is usually warmed before serving, but I actually prefer it chilled, straight from the refrigerator! I like my mother's version of this recipe, because her version is creamier and milkier than what I have seen typically served at restaurants. If you choose to make this a vegan dish and use soy milk, the taste and texture will be a bit different than the traditional version.

1 Using a box grater, shred the carrots on the small grating holes. You should get about 1 cup (100 g) shredded carrots.
2 Pour the milk into a heavy bottomed, medium-sized stockpot. Add the shredded carrots. Bring to a rolling boil over high heat, stirring frequently as it comes to a boil. Reduce the heat to medium.
3 Simmer the milk until it has all cooked off, leaving the carrots in a mushy consistency, stirring occasionally, about 35-45 minutes. If any skin forms, simply stir it back in. If there is any scorched milk on the bottom of the pot, do not scrape it.
4 Add the half-and-half and ½ tablespoon of the almonds. Simmer until all the half-and-half has cooked off, leaving the carrots in a mushy consistency, stirring occasionally, about 5 minutes.
5 Add the sugar and stir until it has all dissolved.
6 Remove from heat and let cool for five minutes, have it now or refrigerate or freeze for later! Before serving, sprinkle the remaining ½ tablespoon almonds and the crushed cardamom seeds on top. This dish will further thicken as it cools, so if you like it extra thick, serve it chilled. If you prefer it a little less thick, serve it warm or reheat it before serving.

Chocolate and Coconut Covered Cherries

I was at a local Indian sweet shop shopping for an assortment of desserts to share with friends when I was hit with an inspiration. I was eyeing the *gulab jamun*, a popular Indian dessert of deep fried dough batter balls, soaked in sugar syrup and then sometimes rolled in coconut flakes, and then the idea came to me. Why not take fresh cherries, pit them, dip them in chocolate, and roll in coconut flakes? So I created this indulgent and beautiful Indian inspired recipe that is now a favorite treat at parties. Cherries boost your memory and are a natural sleep aid, which help regular your sleep cycle to sleep better.

Makes about 15 large or 30 small cherries
Prep time: 25 minutes
Cook time: 2 minutes
Refrigerator life: 3 days

½ lb (225 g) fresh cherries with the stem
  on
¼ lb/4 oz (125 g) chocolate bar
  (dark, bitter-sweet, semi-sweet, or milk
  chocolate)
1¼ cups (125 g) dried, sweetened coconut
  flakes (finely grated or shredded)

> **CHERRY TIP** If at any time the stems falls off, stick it back in the cherry and use some melted chocolate as "glue" and pour it around the top of the cherry where the stem is.

1 Wash the cherries and pat dry with a kitchen towel being careful to not remove the stems. To pit the cherries, hold a cherry in one hand and using a small knife, cut the cherry lengthwise around the pit, making sure not to cut the cherry in half. Gently pry the cherry open with the tips of both of your thumbs and use a thumb tip to pry out the pit, making sure the stem stays in place. The chocolate and coconut will hide the slit in the cherry. It might seem tricky at first, but after pitting a few cherries, it will get easier. Discard the pits. (Cherry juice is very staining so it is a good idea to wear an apron.)

2 Put the coconut flakes in a small bowl. Line a tray with parchment paper. Pat dry the cherries with a paper towel to make sure they are dry.

3 Using your fingers, break the chocolate into small pieces. Place the chocolate in a microwave-safe bowl. Heat the chocolate in the microwave for 1 minute. Stir the chocolate. Heat for an additional 30 seconds. Stir the chocolate. It should be smooth and completely melted. If it is not, heat in the microwave at 30 second intervals, stirring in between, until is it completely melted.

4 Hold a cherry by the stem and dip it into the chocolate. Dip the cherry into the bowl with the coconut flakes. Using your fingers, toss some of the coconut flakes on the cherry so it is generously coated with them. Place the coconut covered cherry on the parchment paper. Repeat with the rest of the cherries.

5 Place the tray in the refrigerator for 30 minutes for the chocolate to set. Enjoy now, or put the cherries in an airtight container and keep in the refrigerator for up to 3 days.

Working with Chocolate:

1 Make sure the cherries are dry before dipping them in the chocolate. If they are wet, the moisture will harden the chocolate and it will be difficult to dip the cherries.

2 Instead of a microwave, you can also easily melt the chocolate on a stovetop using a double boiler. A double boiler is simply a bowl that is set above a pot of simmering water for indirect heat and steam to gently melt the chocolate. **To create a double boiler:** Fill a saucepan halfway with water and bring to a boil over high heat. Reduce the heat to medium-low and place a glass or steel bowl over the saucepan, making sure the bottom of the bowl does not touch the water in the saucepan. If it does, pour out some of the water. Place the chocolate pieces in the bowl. Stir frequently until the chocolate is completely smooth and melted, about 2 minutes. Turn off the heat and remove the bowl from the saucepan. Start dipping the cherries in the melted chocolate.

Index

A

Apple 38, 40
Asparagus spears 38, 44
Avocados 33, 81

B

Baked Whole Wheat Flatbreads 54
Banana 40, 122
Basic Ingredients 24
Basic Techniques 20
Beets 32, 35
Bell Peppers 15, 30, 79, 82, 101, 104, 108
Bitter Melon 94-95
Black Bean Curry 71
Black beans 69, 71
Black-Eyed Pea Curry 72
Black-eyed peas 15, 28, 69, 71, 72
Breads and Rice 52
Broccoli 12, 23, 65, 81
Brussels sprouts 39, 44
Butternut Squash 15, 81, 84
Buttery Black Lentil Stew 75

C

Cabbage 81, 97
Cabbage and Peas 97
Cantaloupe 115, 120,
Carrots 16, 17, 22, 23, 27, 32, 34, 35, 60, 65, 81, 85, 115, 117, 123
Cashews 18, 39, 43, 60, 66
Cauliflower 22, 32, 34, 65, 81, 88
Cauliflower and Potatoes 88
Chai Tea 119
Cheese and Bell Pepper Skewers 108
Cherries 124
Chickpea Curry 78
Chickpeas 8, 69, 73, 75, 78, 79
Chili peppers 19, 23, 25, 30, 34, 35, 36, 46, 50, 75, 76, 78, 79, 81, 98, 107, 111,
Chocolate and Coconut Covered Cherries 124
Chutney 14, 16, 17, 32, 36, 37, 50, 51, 108, 113, 121
Collard greens 12, 15, 81, 99
Collard Greens and Parsnips 99
Corn 45
Creamed Swiss Chard with Cheese Cubes 107
Curried Carrots and Peas 85
Cut Bell Peppers and Potatoes 82

D

Daikon Stuffed Wheat Flatbreads 57
Drinks and Desserts 114

E

Eggplants 8, 12, 13, 21, 81, 96-97
Enjoying Nature's Bounty 12

F

Fenugreek 27, 28, 29, 39, 46-47, 62, 65, 93
Fenugreek and Potatoes 93
Fenugreek Cornbreads 62
Fresh Coriander Chutney 37
Fresh Exotic Fruits 41
Fresh Fruit Juice 117
Fresh Lentil Sprout Salad 79
Fresh Vegetable Juice 117
Fruit Custard 122
Fruitful Ending: Appetizers and Snacks 38

G

Garam Masala 109
Grapefruits 17, 115, 117
Grapes 40, 122
Green Beans 15, 86

Green Beans with Potatoes 86
Green Lentils and Kale Stew 74
Grilled Vegetable Platter 42
Guavas 40

H

Homemade Crumbled Indian Cheese 102
Homemade Garden Tomato Soup 47
Honey dew melon 115, 120

I

Indian Cappuccino 118
Indian Cheese and Pea Curry 106
Indian Cheese Block 104
Indian Cheese with Peas 112
Indian Cornbread 61
Indian Style Grilled Corn 45
Introduction 11

J

Japanese Eggplants with Potatoes 96
Jicama 15, 69, 79,

K

Kale 8, 69, 74
Kidney Bean Curry 70
Kidney beans 28, 69, 70, 71
Kitchen Tools 16

L

Lentils 11, 13, 14, 15, 18, 24, 28, 29, 68, 74, 75, 77, 79,
Lentils and Legumes 68
Locavore 13
Loquats 41
Lychees 41
Mango Ice Cream 121
Mangoes 14, 32, 115, 116, 121

Mashed Turnips 83
Melon Balls in Rose Syrup 120
Mint Rice 67
Mixed Greens 98

O

Okra 12, 15, 21, 69, 81, 92-93,
Opo Squash 12, 18, 21, 28, 32,
    39, 51, 58-59, 73, 81, 95,
Opo Squash Dumpling Curry 95
Opo Squash Flatbreads 58
Opo Squash Fritters 51
Oranges 12, 16, 17, 27, 115, 117,
Oven-Roasted Asparagus Spears
    44

P

Pan-Fried Cheese Cubes 110
Pan-Seared Brussels Sprouts 44
Paneer 11, 16, 19, 30, 87, 101,
    102-103, 104, 107, 110, 112,
Papaya 41
Parsnips 12, 15, 81, 99
Peaches 115, 116
Peanuts 28, 32, 36
Pear 15, 32, 36, 40,
Peas, green 19, 21, 27, 28, 60, 63,
    64, 65, 69, 85, 89, 97, 103, 106,
    112,
Pickled Beets 35
Pickled Carrots 35
Pickled Turnips, Carrots and
    Cauliflower 34
Pickles and Chutneys 32
Pineapples 17, 115, 117
Plain Basmati Rice 63
Plum 40
Pomegranate 40
Pope, Monica 8
Potato Cutlets 50
Potatoes 19, 22, 23, 32-33, 49,
    50, 60, 65, 69, 82, 87, 88, 90,
    93, 96-97, 103

Q

Quinoa 30, 53, 60, 101
Quinoa Cashew Pilaf 60

R

Raita 15, 27, 32-33
Resource Guides 128
Rice with Cumin and Peas 64
Roasted Peanut Chutney 36

S

Saffron, Fruit and Nut Rice 66
Salted Fried Cashews 43
Sautéed Mushrooms and Peas 89
Sautéed Potatoes with Cumin 90
Spiced Fruit Cocktail 40
Spiced Yogurt with Potatoes 32
Spicy Sweet Potatoes 48
Spinach 16, 17, 39, 46-47, 74, 81,
    87, 98, 107, 115, 117
Spinach and Fenugreek Fritters
    46
Spinach and Potatoes 87
Split Chickpea and Zucchini
    Stew 73
Stewed Split Red Lentils 77
Stewed Whole Red Lentils 76
Strawberries 40, 115, 116, 122
Strawberry Lassi 116
Stuffed Bitter Melon 94
Stuffed Okra 92
Sustainable 8, 11, 13
Sweet and Spicy Butternut
    Squash 84
Sweet and Spicy Pear Chutney 36
Sweet potatoes 8, 48-49
Sweetened Carrots 123
Swiss Chard 8, 107

T

Tandoori Tofu Kebabs 113
Tips and Techniques 19

Tofu 11, 13, 14, 15, 19, 24, 27,
    30, 31, 101, 102, 104, 106, 107,
    108, 110-111, 112, 113,
Tofu and Cheese 100
Tofu Breakfast Scramble 111
Turnips 34, 79, 83, 98

V

Vegetable Curry with Tofu 103
Vegetable Main Dishes 80
Vegetable Pilaf Rice 65

W

Watermelon 115, 120

Y

Yellow Squash 14, 91
Yellow Squash Curry 91

Z

Zucchini 39, 42-43, 69, 73

Resource Guides

Visit your famers markets to meet local farmers and get to know your community. Also, on the web, you can visit *localharvest.org* to find your local farmers markets, CSA's, and co-ops. Here are some of my local picks:

All We Need Farm is a small family farm in Needville, TX, a town about an hour southwest of Houston. Stacey Roussel practices organic and chemical-free farming with a focus on returning more to the land than she is taking away. *allweneedfarms.com*

Urban Harvest Farmers Market has four Houston locations. Tyler Horne is the Market Manager. *urbanharvest.org*

Central City Co-op is Houston's organic food co-op in the Heights neighborhood. *centralcityco-op.com*

Farmhouse Delivery, serving Houston and Austin, acts as a farmers market delivered right to your door. The owner, Stephanie Scherzer, is a farmer herself and runs Rain Lily Farms. *farmhousedelivery.com*

Home Sweet Farm, a small CSA farm owned by husband and wife team Brad and Jenny Stufflebeam, is in Brenham, TX. Their beautiful fresh produce is delicious, especially the amazingly bright orange and sweet butternut squash, as I used it to make Sweet and Spicy Butternut Squash Mash (page 84) on Thanksgiving. Monica Pope hosts a weekly pick-up location for their CSA members and also incorporates their produce in her restaurant's weekend menu. *homesweetfarm.com*

Wood Duck Farm, a vendor at Urban Harvest Farmers Market and a CSA, is owned by Van Weldon, New York City trader turned country farmer. Van hosts open houses throughout the year for families to tour his farm. *woodduckfarm.com*

Rawfully Organic, founded by raw vegan Kristina Carrillo-Bucaram, is a non-for-profit organic, raw, and local produce co-op in Houston, TX. *rawfullyorganic.com*

Basketcase is CSA name for Utility Research Garden farm in Jones Creek, an hour south of Houston, TX. It is run by David Cater, who sustainably grows vegetable and fruit varieties from around the world such as daikon, bitter melon, and papaya, as well as greens and root vegetables. *utilityresearchgarden.com*

Blackwood Bounty, the CSA farm located near Hempstead, TX, about 45 minutes northwest of Houston, is run by Hans Hansen whose mission is to provide the highest quality naturally grown vegetables and fruit for the greater Houston area, and to grow relations and community. *blackwoodland.org*

The Tuttle Story: "Books to Span the East and West"

Most people are surprised to learn that the world's largest publisher of books on Asia had its humble beginnings in the tiny American state of Vermont. The company's founder, Charles E. Tuttle, belonged to a New England family steeped in publishing. And his first love was naturally books—especially old and rare editions.

Immediately after WW II, serving in Tokyo under General Douglas MacArthur, Tuttle was tasked with reviving the Japanese publishing industry. He later founded the Charles E. Tuttle Publishing Company, which thrives today as one of the world's leading independent publishers.

Though a westerner, Tuttle was hugely instrumental in bringing a knowledge of Japan and Asia to a world hungry for information about the East. By the time of his death in 1993, Tuttle had published over 6,000 books on Asian culture, history and art—a legacy honored by the Japanese emperor with the "Order of the Sacred Treasure," the highest tribute Japan can bestow upon a non-Japanese.

With a backlist of 1,500 titles, Tuttle Publishing is more active today than at any time in its past—inspired by Charles Tuttle's core mission to publish fine books to span the East and West and provide a greater understanding of each.